The Cookery Year

The Cookery Year

Heather Lambert
Katharine Blakemore

Contents

First published in 1983 by
Octopus Books Limited
59 Grosvenor Street, London W1
Third impression, 1984
© 1983 Hennerwood Publications Limited
ISBN 0 86273 063 5
Printed in Spain by
Artes Graficas Toledo, S.A.
D. L. TO: 65 -1984

Autumn

Winter

Index

The Fruit and Vegetable Year

Main varieties	Source	Availability
Apples		
Culinary		
Grenadier, Lord Derby	United Kingdom	
Dessert		
George Cave, Discovery, Tydemans, Worcester Pearmain, Egremont Russet, Lord Lambourne, Miller's Seedling	United Kingdom	August – October Not normally stored for long period
Culinary		
Bramley	United Kingdom	September – June
Dessert		
Spartan, Cox's Orange Pippin, Ida Red, Laxton Superb, Crispin, Golden Delicious	United Kingdom	October – March and occasionally later
Cox's Orange Pippin, Golden Delicious, Granny Smith, Jonathan, Sturmer Pippin, Democrat, Crofton	Australia	May – August
Jonathan, Red Delicious, Golden Delicious, Granny Smith, Winesap	Argentina	April – June
Cox's Orange Pippin, Golden Delicious	Belgium	November – March
Jonathan	Bulgaria	December
Golden Delicious, McIntosh Red, Red Delicious, Winesap	Canada	November – April
Granny Smith	Chile	April – May
Cox's Orange Pippin, Ida Red, McIntosh Red, Spartan	Denmark	December – March
Golden Delicious, Starcrimson, Granny Smith	France	August – July
Cox's Orange Pippin, Horneburger, Belle de Boskoop	Germany	November
Horneburger, Golden Delicious, Cox's Orange Pippin	Holland	November – March
Jonathan	Hungary	October – January
Belfort, Golden Delicious, Jonathan, Morganduft, Rome Beauty	Italy	October – April
Cox's Orange Pippin, Red Delicious, Red Dougherty, Granny Smith, Gala, Golden Delicious, Sturmer Pippin	New Zealand	April – July
Golden Delicious, Granny Smith, Starking, Top Red	South Africa	March – July
Golden Delicious, Granny Smith	Spain	August – September
Golden Delicious, McIntosh Red, Newtown, Red Delicious, Winesap	USA	December – April
Apricots	Greece, Hungary	June – August
	South Africa	December – February
	Spain	May – August
	Turkey	June – August

Main varieties	Source	Availability
Artichokes		
Globe	Cyprus	January – April
Globe	United Kingdom	June – September
Globe	France	March – November
Globe	Italy	August – October
Globe	Spain	December – June
Jerusalem	United Kingdom	March – July
Asparagus	United Kingdom	May – July
	South Africa	September – January
	Cyprus, France, Israel	January – May
	Kenya	
	USA	
Aubergines	Canary Islands	January – June
	Israel	October – March
	France	March – November
	Holland	February – May
	Italy, Spain	May – September
	Cyprus	May – December
Avocados	Israel	October – May
	Kenya	August – October
	South Africa	March – September
	USA	January – April
Bananas	Canary Islands	All year
	Cameroons	All year
	Dominica	All year
	Jamaica	All year
	Windward Islands	All year
Batavia	Spain	December – January
Beans		
Hot-house	United Kingdom	March – August
Outdoor	United Kingdom	June – September
Runner	United Kingdom	July – October
Broad	United Kingdom	June – July
French	France	November – July
French	Kenya	December – May
French	Canary Islands	March
French	Cyprus	April – November
Broad	France, Italy	April – June
String	France, Spain	May – June
Broad	France, Spain	May – June
Bobi	Italy	June – July
Hot-house	Guernsey	March – August
Beetroot	United Kingdom	All year
	Cyprus, Italy	March – July
Blackcurrants	United Kingdom	June – August
Brussels sprouts	United Kingdom	August – April
	Holland	June – March
Cabbage		
January King	United Kingdom	October – April
Drumhead	United Kingdom	August – November
Spring Green	United Kingdom	November – March
Primo	United Kingdom	June – August
Red	United Kingdom	December – February
White, Red	Holland	September – June
Capsicums	Canary Islands	April – August; December
	Cyprus	June – August
	Egypt	March
	France	June – December
	Israel	October – June
	Italy	July – October
	Kenya	February – June
	Cuba	October – November
	Ethiopia	April – May

Main varieties	Source	Availability
Carrots	United Kingdom	All year (break May – June)
	Holland	All year
	Canada, Cyprus, France, Italy, USA	February – July
	Israel	April – June
Cauliflower/ Broccoli	United Kingdom	All year broccoli
	France, Italy, Jersey	November – April
	Holland	June
Celeriac	United Kingdom	September – March
	France	September – December
Celery	United Kingdom	June – February
	Israel, USA	January – July
Cherries	United Kingdom	June – August
	Cyprus	June – August
	Canada	April – July
	France, Italy, Spain	May – June
	USA	July – August
	New Zealand	July – February
	France	September – October
Chicory	Belgium	September – June
Chillies	Canary Islands	March – July
	Cyprus	May – November
	France	June – February
	Kenya	July
Chinese leaf	Israel	December – April
Clementines	Spain	November – February
	Cyprus, Morocco, Corsica	December – February
Corn-on-the-cob	United Kingdom	August – October
	France, Italy	July – August
	Israel, Spain	February – April
	USA	August – September
Courgettes	United Kingdom	June – September
	France	May – June; October – June
	Canary Islands	January
	East Africa, Ethiopia, Jersey	June – July
	Cyprus	March – June; October – December
	Israel	January – June
Cranberries	USA	December – January
Cucumbers	United Kingdom	March – October
	Canary Islands	November – March
	Cyprus	March – August
	Holland	March – December
Custard apples	Madeira	September – February
Damsons	United Kingdom	August – October
Dates	Tunis	September – March
	Iraq	October – December
	Israel (Fresh)	All year
Endive	United Kingdom	May – August
	France	September – May
	Italy	February
	Spain	January – March
Fennel	France	October – January
	Italy	June – March

Main varieties	Source	Availability
Figs	France	September – November
	Greece	October – December
	Turkey	November – December
Garlic	France	All year
	Italy	August – March
	Portugal	February – March
Gooseberries	Hungary	June
	United Kingdom	June – August
Granadillas	Madeira	November
Grapefruit	Brazil	April – August
	Cuba, Honduras	September – November
	Cyprus	December – April
	Israel	October – July
	Jamaica	June – October
	Dominica	November – December
	Paraguay	April – July
	South Africa	April – October
	Spain, Surinam	September – November
	Trinidad, USA	October – April
Grapes Colmar, Muscat, Royal	Belgium	October – December June – August, November
Italia, Violet Purple	Brazil	November – March
Almeria, Red Emperor	Chile	May
Rozaki, Seedless, Cardinal, Sultana	Cyprus	June – September
Alphonse Lavalle	France	August – October
Alphonse Lavalle, Perlette, Sultana, Waltham Cross	Israel	June – July
Regina	Italy	July – August
Sweet Water	Portugal	July – October
Almeria, Alphonse Lavalle, Barlinka, Golden Hill, New Cross, Dan-ben-Hannah, Waltham Cross, Queen of the Vineyard, Salba	South Africa	January – June
Almeria	Spain	October – January
Almeria	Turkey	September
Red Emperor	USA	October – January
Greengages	United Kingdom, Italy	July – August
	Spain, France	June – August
Kiwifruit Hayward	New Zealand	June – December
Leeks	United Kingdom, Ireland	August – April
Lemons	Cyprus	August – April
	Greece	October – December
	Israel	March – June
	Spain	All year
	USA	All year
	Italy	All year
	South Africa	All year

The Fruit and Vegetable Year

Main varieties	Source	Availability
Lettuce		
Indoor and outdoor	United Kingdom	All year
	France	December – April
	Holland	October – June
	Italy, Spain	February – May
	Jersey	May – August
Iceberg	Israel	December – April
Cos	Cyprus	December – May
Limes	South Africa, West Indies	July – October
Loganberries	United Kingdom	July – August
Lychees	South Africa	December – February
Mandarins (soft citrus types)	Spain	October – April
	Italy, Israel	December – May
	Morocco	October – February
	South Africa	June – September
Mangoes	Brazil	All year
	India	May – July
	Kenya	January – September
Marrows	United Kingdom	June – October
	Cyprus	April – July
Medlars	United Kingdom	November
	Cyprus	April – May
Melons		
Green Honeydew	Argentina	February – June
	Brazil	November – March
Ogen	Canary Islands	June – August
Black Tendral	Chile	February – June
Honeydew, White Water	Cyprus	July – September
Charentais	France	June – September
Net, Tiger	Holland	July – September
Ogen, Galia	Israel	April – January
Water, Honeydew	Israel	May – August
White	South Africa	December – May
Charentais, Ogen, Water, Green Honeydew, Yellow	Spain	March – December
Mint	United Kingdom	October – January
Mushrooms	United Kingdom, Eire	All year
Mustard and cress	United Kingdom	All year
Nectarines	Belgium	May
	South Africa	December – March
	USA	August – September
Okra	Kenya, Morocco	June – September
	Cyprus	June – October
Onions	United Kingdom	September – January
	Canada, Hungary, Italy, Poland, USA	August – May
	Cape, Chile, Egypt	February – July
	Canary Islands, Holland	May – April
	Israel	May – June
	Spain	All year

Main varieties	Source	Availability
Oranges		
Navels	Australia	April – May
Navels	Brazil	April – December
Ovals	Cyprus	December – April
Valencia Lates	Cyprus	March – April
Jaffa Shamoutis	Israel	December – April
Navels	Israel	November – December
Valencia Lates	Israel	April – June
Palermo Bitters	Italy	January – February
Hamlins	Morocco	January
Navels, Valencia Lates	Morocco	January – June
Navels, Valencia Lates	South Africa	May – September
Bloods	Spain	February – May
Blonds, Cadeneras	Spain	January – March
Navels, Navelinas	Spain	November – April
Seville Bitters	Spain	December – February
Valencia Lates, Vernas	Spain	April – July
Navels	USA	April – September
Ortaniques	Jamaica	January – April
Parsley	United Kingdom	April – January
	France	January – May
	Jersey	November – February
Parsnips	United Kingdom	September – April
Passion fruit	Kenya, Madeira	January – March
Peaches		
Armagold, Cardinal, Dixie Red, Fairhaven, Hales, Southland	Canada	October
	Greece	September
	France, Italy, Spain	June – September
Culemborg, Peregrine, Rhodes, Van Riebeeck	South Africa	December – March
Various	Turkey	August – October
	USA	April – May
Pears		
Clapps Favourite, Comice, Conference	United Kingdom	August – March
Williams	United Kingdom	August – September
Anjou, Beurré Hardy, Williams, Winter Nelis	Argentina	February – April
Anjou, Beurré Bosc, Comice, Josephine, Packham's, Williams, Winter Cole, Winter Nelis	Australia	March – July
Dr Jules, Guyot, Passacrassane, Williams	France	August – October
Beurré Hardy, Conference	Holland	November – February
Passacrassana	Italy	February – March
Williams	Italy	July – October
Packham's, Williams, Winter Cole, Winter Nelis	New Zealand	March – June
Bon Chrétien, Buerré Bosc, Beurré Hardy, Comice, Packham's, Winter Nelis	South Africa	January – June
Guyot, Williams	Spain	July – September

Main varieties	Source	Availability
Peas	United Kingdom Cyprus East Africa France	May – October March – April April – November May – August
Pineapples Red Spanish	Kenya	All year
Cayenne Ivory Coast	South Africa South Africa	All year October – January
Plums Belle de Louvain, Bush, Czars, Droopers, Monarch, Quillins Gage, Pershore, Pond's, Switchen, Victoria	United Kingdom	June – October
President	Argentina	April – May
Switchen	Bulgaria	August – October
Switchen	Hungary	August – October
Florentia, Gaviota, Santa Rosa	Italy	June – July
Switzen	Yugoslavia	August – September
Gaviota, Harry Pickstone, Golden King, Kelsey, Santa Rosa, Songold	South Africa	December – April
Formosa, Gage, Santa Rosa	Spain	July
Santa Rosa	USA	September – October
Victoria type, Belle de Louvain	France	August
Pomegranates	Cyprus, Israel, Spain	September – November
Potatoes New	United Kingdom Belgium, Cyprus, Egypt, Greece, Israel, Italy, Jersey, Spain France Canary Islands, Italy, Morocco Guernsey Malta	June – July March – July June November – June January – April April – August
Ware	United Kingdom Holland	August onwards
Pumpkins	United Kingdom Italy	August – October June – July
Radishes	United Kingdom Guernsey, Israel Holland USA	April – October December – June March October – January
Raspberries	United Kingdom South Africa, New Zealand	June – September December
Red Currants	United Kingdom	June – August
Rhubarb Forced Outdoor	United Kingdom United Kingdom	December – March March – June
Salsify	Belgium France	October – June October

Main varieties	Source	Availability
Satsumas	Spain	October – February
Seakale	United Kingdom	December – March
Soft Citrus Michal	Israel	November – December
Clementine Orlando, Dancy Mineola, Wilking Temple Topaz	Israel Israel Israel Israel Israel	December January January – February February – March April – May
Spinach	United Kingdom France Cyprus	April – November November – April October – April
Strawberries Cloche Outdoor	United Kingdom United Kingdom Cyprus, France Greece, Guernsey, Holland, Jersey, Spain, USA, Italy, Israel, Kenya, New Zealand	April – June May – October February – June September – May
Swedes	United Kingdom	September – May
Sweet potatoes	Canary Islands USA	September – June January – March
Tomatoes	United Kingdom Canary Islands Guernsey Holland, Jersey, Spain, Morocco, France, Cyprus, Israel	April – October October – May March – November April – October October – January
Turnips	United Kingdom France	All year April – June
Watercress	United Kingdom	All year

By kind permission of the National Institute of Fresh Produce

Spring

I am sure that springtime must be nearly everyone's favourite season of the year. There is nothing more guaranteed to put us all in a good mood than seeing the first crocuses or watching the daffodils bend their heads and open out during March or early April. Then later on in the spring we have the wonderful sight of the azaleas, camellias and rhododendrons.

FLOWER ARRANGEMENTS

If you are lucky enough to have camellias in your garden, you could pick one or two of the blossoms, shorten the stems to about one inch and float them in a shallow bowl as a table centre. You can also make very pretty table arrangements with daffodils but remember that they do not last long in the house, especially if you have central heating. If you pick or buy them just as the buds are coming out on the day before entertaining, they will be at their best by the following day.

FRUIT AND VEGETABLES

We still have to rely very much on imported fruit and vegetables from all over the world and prices remain high. Winter English greens such as cabbage, sprouts, leeks, seakale and spinach are still around in early spring, as are many of the root vegetables such as carrots, Jerusalem artichokes, beetroot, parsnips and swedes. We also have English fruits available from store, such as cooking and eating apples, as well as certain varieties of pears. Then we have our own rhubarb and, later on, gooseberries.

Of the many imported vegetables and fruits in the shops, my favourites are the new potatoes. Those from Egypt, the Canary Islands and Cyprus are the best value for money – the Jersey potatoes are wonderful to eat, but always expensive by comparison.

HOME FREEZING

Home freezing is very much the fashion at the moment. Gardeners have become aware of the joys of freezing their own vegetables, and for those who live in towns, a day out to the local 'pick your own' centres has become very popular. This is not only a pleasant outing for the family at the weekend, but it also keeps the housekeeping budget down.

THE MENUS

Although spring officially starts in March, it can be a very cold month, and hot nourishing food is still welcome, but as we progress into April and May, we begin to appreciate light menus and some cold food as part of the daily diet.

The Easter tea and May buffet are planned for special occasions, for twelve people, but all the recipes can be doubled or trebled if you find that you have a larger number of guests. The May buffet is particularly planned for a family wedding, birthday or anniversary.

MEAT

Meat in general does not have any season, with the exception of lamb. The first English spring lamb is available in the shops in March. The meat is very pale and sweet, and the fat has not had time to build up. This is when a shoulder of lamb really comes into its own. Good roasting pork also takes careful choosing if you like the crackling. There is no actual season for pork but the best is usually available in April and May. Choose a joint with a nice pale skin, and get your butcher to score it. Rub plenty of salt between the scores – this 'irritates' during the cooking to help the skin to crackle – then rub in plenty of cooking oil. Cook the pork at a high temperature until the crackling is set, then lower the oven heat to complete the cooking.

CHEESE

The choosing of cheese for the last course of a dinner menu is always difficult, especially as there are so many different varieties in the shops these days. Cheese is always an expensive item, and the temptation is to buy too many different kinds, which only leads to waste, since guests tend to take a little of each one and you are left with lots of small offcuts. If you do find yourself in this situation, you can blend cheese into dressings (see Three Cheese Dressing, page 48), or use them up in flans.

A wide variety of cheeses from all over the world are now available country-wide. We all know about our classic British cheeses, such as Cheddar, Stilton, Red Leicester, Caerphilly, Double Gloucester, and the traditional French cheeses, such as Camembert and Brie, but now is the time to become more adventurous. All good chain supermarkets stock a wide variety of cheeses – especially from France. Why not try Roquefort or Bleu d'Auvergne – two lovely blue cheeses from central France – or goats' cheese wrapped in vine leaves from Provence? The choice is endless.

For a normal dinner party of 6-8 people a choice of three cheeses is sufficient. Choose one hard English cheese, then one blue cheese and finally a cream texture cheese. Cheese should not be eaten straight from the refrigerator, so unwrap the pieces and arrange them on a cheese board with a garnish of parsley or grapes and cover lightly with cling wrap, then set aside at room temperature for about two hours.

HERBS

Finally, let us not forget that spring is the time of year to plant herbs. You do not have to possess a garden for this as many of the smaller herbs can be grown in window boxes or tubs. Study the backs of the seed packets carefully when buying as the information given will tell you when to plant and how high the herbs will grow. There are also some very attractive herb charts on the market which you can hang on your kitchen wall.

Lunch or Supper
MARCH

CREAM OF CAULIFLOWER SOUP
WITH PARMESAN FLORETS

OEUFS MOLLETS WITH TOAST

FRUIT SALAD AND CREAM

Cream of Cauliflower Soup with Parmesan Florets

SERVES 6

50 g (2 oz) butter
1 large cauliflower, trimmed and cut into florets
450 g (1 lb) potatoes, peeled and thinly sliced
1.2 litres (2 pints) chicken stock
1 garlic clove, peeled and crushed (optional)
2 sprigs parsley
1 bay leaf
salt
freshly ground black pepper
1 x 150 ml (5 fl oz) carton single cream

TO GARNISH:

15 g (½ oz) butter
20 miniature florets, reserved from the cauliflower
1 tablespoon grated Parmesan cheese
chopped fresh parsley

PREPARATION TIME: *20 minutes*

COOKING TIME: *1 hour 10 minutes*

1. Melt the butter in a large saucepan and add the cauliflower, setting aside 1 large floret split into 20 miniature ones for the garnish.

2. Add the potatoes and stir over a low heat to make sure that the vegetables are well coated with butter.

3. Cover the pan and sweat the contents for about 5 minutes, stirring occasionally.

4. Pour over the stock and add the garlic, if using, parsley, bay leaf, salt and pepper. Replace the lid and simmer gently for 45 minutes.

5. Cool the soup a little, removing the parsley sprigs and bay leaf, then pass it through a liquidizer, food processor or sieve, blending well until the texture is creamy and smooth.

6. Rinse the pan and return the soup to the heat. Bring slowly to boiling point.

7. Meanwhile, make the Parmesan florets. Melt the butter for the garnish in a small pan and fry the florets quickly until crisp. Drain them, then toss in Parmesan cheese.

8. To serve, stir the cream into the soup and pour into the soup tureen. Sprinkle the Parmesan florets and parsley over the top.

Oeufs Mollets

SERVES 6

50 g (2 oz) butter
1 medium onion, diced
1 red pepper, diced
1 green pepper, diced
100 g (4 oz) ham, diced
100 g (4 oz) button
  mushrooms, sliced
salt
freshly ground black pepper
6 eggs
1 x 150 ml (5 fl oz) carton
  single cream
hot buttered toast, to serve

PREPARATION TIME: *25 minutes*

COOKING TIME: *30 minutes*

OVEN: *150°C, 300°F, Gas Mark 2*

This recipe is based on a classic French dish. Any variety of vegetables may be used for the macédoine base, and the amount of time in the oven entirely depends on how long you like your eggs cooked.

1. Melt the butter in a saucepan and add the onion and peppers. Allow to cook gently in the butter, without browning, for 2 minutes.
2. Add the ham, mushrooms, salt and pepper, and cook for a further 5-7 minutes, stirring gently.
3. Spoon the vegetable mixture into a greased gratin dish or into 6 individual ovenproof dishes, and make 6 holes in this mixture.
4. Break the eggs into the holes, and pour a little cream over each one.
5. Bake in a preheated oven for approximately 15 minutes for individual dishes and 25-30 minutes if using 1 large dish. Serve with hot buttered toast.

Evening Meal
(MARCH)

PIPERADE STUFFED COURGETTES

BUTTERY FRIED FILLETS OF PLAICE
WITH FRIED PARSLEY

GLAZED CARROTS

BAKED POTATOES

CITRUS FLAN

Piperade Stuffed Courgettes

SERVES 6

*6 courgettes approximately
   13 cm (5 inches) in length*
50 g (2 oz) butter
*1 medium onion, peeled and
   finely chopped*
*1 red pepper, cored and finely
   chopped*
*75 g (3 oz) frozen peas,
   blanched*
1 teaspoon dried dill weed
2 tablespoons single cream
salt
freshly ground black pepper
4 eggs, beaten

PREPARATION TIME: *20 minutes*

COOKING TIME: *20 minutes*

Courgettes are available all
the year round now. During
March they come mostly
from Cyprus or Israel. They
are picked when very young
and tender, so they are
perfect for this pretty dish.
Try to select evenly-sized
courgettes for the most
attractive presentation. The
dish may be served hot or
cold. If serving the dish hot,
keep the courgettes warm
while making the filling, and
serve at once.

1. Top and tail the
courgettes, and plunge them
into a pan of boiling salted
water. Cook until just tender
when pricked with a knife,
about 8 minutes, then drain
them and refresh them under
a cold tap for a few minutes to
set the colour.
2. Split the courgettes
lengthways, scoop out the
centres and discard.
3. To make the filling, melt
the butter in a frying pan and
add the onion and red
pepper. Cook gently, without
colouring, until soft. Add the
peas to the pan.
4. Beat the dill weed, cream,
salt and freshly ground black
pepper into the eggs, and
pour into the pan of
vegetables.
5. Stir gently until the eggs
are lightly scrambled in the
vegetable mixture. Remove
from the heat.
6. Arrange the halved
courgettes in a serving dish
and fill each one with the egg
and vegetable mixture.
7. Serve immediately with
toast or French bread, or
serve cold with granary bread
and butter.

Buttery Fried Fillets of Plaice with Fried Parsley

SERVES 6

6 fillets of plaice
flour, for coating
salt
freshly ground black pepper
175 g (6 oz) butter
12 large parsley sprigs

PREPARATION TIME: *10 minutes*

COOKING TIME: *20 minutes*

This is a simple French method of frying any white fish. You will find that the butter will go very dark brown when frying the parsley, this is known as 'beurre noir' (black butter) in France, and gives a delicious flavour to the fish. Capers may be added to the parsley, but they are not very popular with children.

1. Trim away any bones from the fillets of plaice, (a fishmonger in a hurry often leaves some little bones at the head end). Season the flour with salt and pepper, then dip the fillets in it.

2. Melt half the butter in a large frying pan, and fry the fillets for about 3 minutes on each side. If they are very large they may take a little longer.

3. Add more of the butter as you fry, as the flour-coated fish tends to soak up the fat. Keep the cooked fish warm on a serving platter.

4. When all 6 fillets are cooked, add any remaining butter to the pan and raise the heat. Add the parsley, and toss in the butter over a high heat until it becomes crispy. This will take 3-4 minutes.

5. Pour the parsley and juices over the fish and serve immediately, accompanied by glazed carrots and baked potatoes.

Citrus Flan

SERVES 6

PASTRY:
150 g (5 oz) plain flour, sifted
75 g (3 oz) butter, cut into
* small chunks*
50 g (2 oz) caster sugar
2 egg yolks

FRENCH CUSTARD BASE:
300 ml (½ pint) milk
1 vanilla pod
65 g (2½ oz) caster sugar
3 egg yolks
10 g (¼ oz) flour
10 g (¼ oz) cornflour

FILLING:
3 oranges, peeled and
* segmented*
3 lemons, peeled and
* segmented*
2 grapefruit, peeled
* and segmented*

GLAZE:
2 tablespoons apricot jam,
* sieved*
2 tablespoons water

PREPARATION TIME: *40 minutes*

COOKING TIME: *40 minutes*

OVEN: *180°C, 350°F, Gas Mark 4*

1. Make the pastry case. Place the flour on a board or marble slab, and make a well in the centre. Put the butter, caster sugar and yolks into the well, then gradually work all the ingredients together until they form a stiff dough. Knead gently until smooth.
2. Use the dough to line a 20 cm (8 inch) fluted flan case. Prick the base and bake blind in a preheated oven for about 20 minutes until lightly browned. Remove from the oven and allow to cool in the tin, leaving the oven on.
3. Meanwhile, make up the custard base. Bring the milk and vanilla pod gently to the boil in a heavy saucepan.
4. Cream the sugar and yolks in a mixing bowl until light and fluffy, then sift the flour and cornflour into this mixture and fold in gently.
5. Remove the vanilla pod from the milk, and pour it over the egg and flour mixture, whisking vigorously. Rinse the milk pan and strain in the custard mixture. Whisk over the heat until the mixture thickens.
6. Allow to cool, then spread it over the pastry base.
7. Arrange the fruit segments overlapping on top of the custard, using the grapefruit on the outside, then the orange, and the lemon in the centre.
8. Melt the apricot jam in the water in a small saucepan. Bring to the boil, then use to glaze the flan.
9. Return to the oven and cook for 15-20 minutes, or until the top is lightly browned. Serve hot or cold.

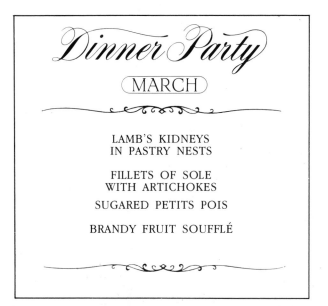

Dinner Party

(MARCH)

LAMB'S KIDNEYS
IN PASTRY NESTS

FILLETS OF SOLE
WITH ARTICHOKES

SUGARED PETITS POIS

BRANDY FRUIT SOUFFLÉ

Lamb's Kidneys in Pastry Nests

SERVES 6

PASTRY NESTS:
225 g (8 oz) shortcrust pastry

FILLING:
40 g (1½ oz) butter
1 medium onion, peeled and finely chopped
1 garlic clove, peeled and crushed
6 lamb's kidneys, peeled, cored and thinly sliced
15 g (½ oz) flour
150 ml (¼ pint) white wine
150 ml (¼ pint) stock
50 g (2 oz) button mushrooms, sliced
1 tablespoon chopped fresh parsley
2 tomatoes, skinned, pipped and diced
salt
freshly ground black pepper
parsley sprigs, to garnish

PREPARATION TIME: *30 minutes*
COOKING TIME: *45 minutes*
OVEN: *190°C, 375°F, Gas Mark 5*

1. To make the pastry nests, roll out the shortcrust pastry and use to line 6 individual foil containers (or ramekin dishes) each 6 cm (2½ inches) in diameter and 2.5 cm (1 inch) deep.
2. Line the pastry cases with greaseproof paper, then fill them with dried peas or lentils.
3. Bake blind in a preheated oven for 10 minutes.
4. Remove the paper with the peas or lentils, and return the pastry cases to the oven for 6-10 minutes until light golden in colour. Allow to cool then unmould.
5. To make the filling, melt the butter in a large shallow pan, and add the onion and garlic. Allow to cook gently until pale golden in colour. Add the kidneys to the pan, raise the heat and fry, stirring, for 2-3 minutes.
6. Remove the pan from the heat and stir in the flour, then the wine, stock, mushrooms and parsley. Return to the heat and simmer, stirring gently, for 8-10 minutes.
7. Add the tomatoes and salt and pepper, just allowing time for the tomatoes to warm through without breaking up.
8. When ready to serve, warm the pastry cases through and fill with the kidney mixture. Garnish with sprigs of parsley.

VARIATION:
For a less expensive dish, gently poach some smoked haddock and a little cod in milk. Reserve the cooking liquid and bone and flake the fish. Make a thick white sauce with the cooking liquid, then gently fold in the flaked fish. Fill the nests, sprinkle with a little grated cheddar cheese, and place in a moderate oven for 10-15 minutes before serving.

Fillets of Sole with Artichokes

SERVES 6

6 large fillets of lemon sole,
    skinned
300 ml (½ pint) milk
6 peppercorns
sprig of parsley
6 slices of carrot
1 shallot, peeled and sliced
1 bay leaf
salt

FOR THE BASE:
6 medium waxy potatoes,
    peeled and thinly sliced
50 g (2 oz) butter
2 tablespoons oil
2 x 175 g (6 oz) cans artichoke
    hearts, drained and
    quartered

SAUCE:
25 g (1 oz) butter
25 g (1 oz) flour
250 ml (8 fl oz) strained fish
    liquor
120 ml (4 fl oz) single cream
1 tablespoon chopped fresh
    parsley
salt
freshly ground black pepper
lemon wedges, to garnish

PREPARATION TIME: *45 minutes*

COOKING TIME: *about 45
    minutes*

OVEN: *160°C, 325°F, Gas Mark 3*

1. To cook the fish, roll up the fillets and place in a lightly buttered gratin dish. Pour over the milk, and add the peppercorns, parsley sprig, carrot, shallot, bay leaf and a little salt.
2. Cover the dish with foil and bake in a preheated oven for 25-30 minutes.
3. Remove the fish rolls and keep warm and covered. Strain off 250 ml (8 fl oz) of the fish liquor for the sauce.
4. While the fish is cooking make up the base. Dry the sliced potatoes in a clean tea towel, then melt the butter and oil in a frying pan and briskly fry the chips until lightly browned on either side. Remove from the pan with a slotted spoon and keep warm.
5. Add the artichoke hearts and toss in the hot fat for 4-5 minutes.
6. Mix the potatoes and artichokes together and place them in the base of a large gratin dish.
7. To make the sauce, melt the butter in a saucepan and add the flour. Cook the roux for 2-3 minutes, stirring constantly, then remove from the heat and gradually incorporate the fish liquor.
8. Return the pan to the heat and bring slowly to the boil, stirring all the time. Allow to simmer for 3-4 minutes.
9. Remove from the heat and stir in the cream. Carefully add salt and pepper to taste.
10. Arrange the fish rolls in a line over the artichoke and potato mixture and pour over the sauce. Garnish the dish with lemon wedges. Serve with Sugared petit pois (see right).

NOTE:
At certain times of the year the soles tend to be smaller, so you might need 3 or even 4 fillets per head.

Sugared Petits Pois

SERVES 6

50 g (2 oz) butter
750 g (1½ lb) frozen petits pois
2 sprigs fresh mint, or 1
    teaspoon dried mint
salt
freshly ground black pepper
1 teaspoon sugar

PREPARATION TIME: *5 minutes*

COOKING TIME: *10-15 minutes*

Young peas cooked in butter and mint with a touch of sugar are delicious. Young sprigs of mint should be growing well in the garden, and similarly should be available in the shops by this time of year.

1. Melt the butter in a large saucepan, then add the peas and mint, salt, pepper and sugar.
2. Cover the saucepan and gently allow the peas to sweat in the butter over a low heat until tender. It is very important to keep the heat low, otherwise the peas will begin to fry in the butter.
3. Without uncovering, toss the pan from time to time to ensure even cooking.
4. Turn into a vegetable dish and serve.

VARIATION:
If you are unable to obtain the fresh mint, use recently purchased dried mint.

Brandy Fruit Soufflé

SERVES 6

3 tablespoons redcurrant jelly
2 tablespoons brandy
75 g (3 oz) mixed dried fruit
25 g (1 oz) mixed peel
4 egg whites
175 g (6 oz) caster sugar
single cream, to serve

PREPARATION TIME: *15 minutes,*
plus cooling

COOKING TIME: *25-30 minutes*

OVEN: *150°C, 300°F, Gas Mark 2*

This soufflé can be put in the oven as you serve your main course. It can be kept in a warm oven for at least 20 minutes after cooking without subsiding.

1. Place the redcurrant jelly, brandy, mixed fruit and mixed peel in a small pan, and melt gently over a low heat, stirring occasionally. Set aside to cool.
2. Grease and sugar a 15 cm (6 inch) soufflé dish, and set aside.
3. Whisk the egg whites until very stiff, then, using a metal spoon, fold in the sugar and fruit mixture.
4. Turn into the soufflé dish and make peaks on the top with the back of a spoon.
5. Bake in a preheated oven for 25-30 minutes, until risen and lightly browned.
6. Serve hot with single cream in a separate jug.

Easter High Tea
APRIL

OPEN SANDWICHES

TRIPLE DECKER SANDWICHES

CURRIED PRAWN TARTLETS

ALMOND SCONES

SPICED YEAST BUNS

SIMNEL CAKE

RHUBARB AND GINGER JAM

BANANA TEA LOAF

Most of the recipes included in the Easter high tea can be made in advance and placed in the deep freeze. All the family need that four day holiday after the cold days and dark evenings of the early months of the year, so the more you can make in advance, the less time you will need to spend cooking.

The Simnel cake itself may be made up to 4 weeks in advance, then stored in a tin or airtight container. The top layer of marzipan and the decoration should not be put on until the Thursday of Easter week, as this will dry out and crack in storage.

CLOCKWISE FROM THE TOP:
Simnel cake (recipe page 26); Open sandwiches;
Triple decker sandwiches (recipes page 24).
MIDDLE: *Curried prawn tartlets (recipe page 24)*

Ideas for Open Sandwiches and Triple Decker Sandwiches

Open sandwiches have come to this country from Scandinavia, where they are the basis of a 'Smorgasbord' or cold buffet. They look very attractive on the table, but are not always popular with children, whereas they seem to prefer the look of the triple deckers.

THREE OPEN SANDWICHES:
1. Lightly scramble some eggs and allow to cool. Stir in some chopped smoked salmon pieces and season with a little salt and plenty of black pepper. Add a little cream if the consistency is too firm. Spread this mixture thickly on to slices of buttered black bread, which is available at any good delicatessen throughout the country. Garnish with fresh or dried dill weed.
2. Butter slices of toasted white bread with crusts removed, then place a slice of rare roast beef on each piece of toast. Top the beef with cottage cheese and chives, and decorate with a sprinkling of paprika pepper and a sprig of parsley.
3. Cover buttered slices of granary bread with a thin layer of cream cheese, then cover with thin slices of fresh or tinned pineapple. Place 2 small rolls of smoked ham on top, then garnish with sieved hard-boiled egg and a gherkin fan. (Pictured on page 23.)

TRIPLE DECKERS:
Triple decker sandwiches consist of 3 layers of bread instead of the usual 2. Choose firm fillings (in contrasting colours), otherwise the sandwich will squash together when the crusts are removed. Alternate the layers by using brown and white thinly sliced bread.

SUGGESTED FILLINGS:
1. A layer of cucumber and a layer of mashed tuna fish.
2. A layer of potted crabmeat and a layer of cress.
3. A layer of cottage cheese and a layer of ham.
4. A layer of mashed banana and a layer of brown sugar.

Stand the sandwiches upright and garnish with parsley or watercress, if liked. (Pictured on page 22.)

Curried Prawn Tartlets

MAKES 20

50 g (2 oz) butter
50 g (2 oz) plain flour
2 teaspoons curry paste or curry powder
600 ml (1 pint) milk
few drops anchovy essence
450 g (1 lb) peeled prawns, less 20 for garnishing
salt
freshly ground black pepper
1 x 375 g (13 oz) packed frozen shortcrust pastry, thawed

TO GARNISH:
20 peeled prawns
paprika pepper
20 small sprigs parsley

PREPARATION TIME: *20 minutes, plus cooling*

COOKING TIME: *35 minutes*

OVEN: *190°C, 375°F, Gas Mark 5*

These tartlets are equally nice served warm.

1. Melt the butter in a pan, then stir in the flour and curry paste or powder. Cook the roux for 2-3 minutes.
2. Remove the pan from the heat and gradually incorporate the milk.
3. Return the sauce to the heat, and bring gently to simmering point, stirring all the time. Simmer for 4-5 minutes. Add a little anchovy essence, then pour the sauce into a mixing bowl and cover with cling film while cooling, to prevent a skin forming.
4. Meanwhile, roll out the pastry, and cut out 20 circles, using a 7.5 cm (3 inch) fluted pastry cutter.
5. Place the circles in tartlet tins, prick the bases, and bake blind in a preheated oven for about 15-20 minutes, until crisp and light golden in colour. Cool on a wire tray.
6. When the sauce is cold, stir in the prawns, and add a little salt and pepper. Fill the tartlets with this mixture, garnish with the reserved prawns, sprinkle with a little paprika, and add a sprig of parsley to each one. (Pictured on page 23.)

Almond Scones

MAKES 10

175 g (6 oz) plain flour
½ teaspoon salt
4 teaspoons baking powder
2 tablespoons ground almonds
50 g (2 oz) butter, cut into chunks
50 g (2 oz) sultanas
150 ml (¼ pint) milk
few drops almond essence
milk, to glaze

PREPARATION TIME: *15 minutes*

COOKING TIME: *10 minutes*

OVEN: *200°C, 400°F, Gas Mark 6*

These scones are delicious to eat just simply buttered, or you can make a real Devon tea out of them by spreading with butter, then strawberry jam, and topping with clotted or lightly whipped double cream.

1. Sift the flour, salt and baking powder together in a bowl, then stir in the ground almonds.
2. Add the butter, and rub it in until the mixture resembles fine breadcrumbs, then stir in the sultanas.
3. Make a well in the centre of the mixture, and pour in the milk and almond essence. Mix lightly with a wooden spoon or fork until a soft dough is formed.
4. Turn the dough on to a floured board and knead gently until smooth. Roll out the dough to 1 cm (½ inch) thick and cut into rounds with a 6 cm (2½ inch) cutter.
5. Place the scones on a lightly greased baking sheet, and brush the tops gently with milk.
6. Bake in a preheated oven for 7-10 minutes, or until the scones are well risen and golden brown. Remove from the oven and cool on a wire tray.

Spiced Yeast Buns

MAKES 24

450 g (1 lb) plain flour
½ teaspoon salt
1 teaspoon ground cinnamon
1 tablespoon sugar
75 g (3 oz) lard, cut into
*   chunks*
10 g (¼ oz) dried yeast
275 ml (9 fl oz) tepid milk
2 eggs, beaten

GLAZE:

1 tablespoon water
1 tablespoon caster sugar
extra sugar, for dredging

PREPARATION TIME: *20 minutes,*
*   plus rising*

COOKING TIME: *10-15 minutes*

OVEN: *220°C, 425°F, Gas Mark 7*

1. Warm a large mixing bowl and sift in the flour, salt and cinnamon.
2. Rub in the lard until the mixture resembles fine breadcrumbs, then stir in the sugar.
3. Cream the yeast with a little of the warm milk, then return this mixture to the remaining milk. Add the beaten eggs to the milk and mix together well.
4. Make a well in the centre of the flour, and add the milk mixture, incorporating it slowly until a dough is formed.
5. Turn on to a floured board and knead for 10 minutes, then return to the mixing bowl, cover with a clean teatowel and put in a warm place to rise until the dough has doubled in bulk.
6. Knock back the dough and divide into 24 pieces. Shape each piece into a sausage about 9 cm (3½ inches) in length and 2.5 cm (1 inch) in diameter.
7. Place the buns on a baking sheet fairly close together, so that they join up during cooking.
8. Prove in a warm place for15 minutes, then bake in a preheated oven for 10-15 minutes.
9. While the buns are cooking place the water and sugar in a small pan, and boil together until a light syrup is formed.
10. As soon as the buns are cooked, brush them with the syrup, then dredge with caster sugar. Serve with Rhubarb and Ginger Jam (see page 26).

VARIATION:

If using fresh yeast to make this recipe, weigh out 15 g (½ oz) and place it in a small mixing bowl. Add 1 teaspoon of sugar and mix well together with a small spoon. The mixture will become runny, which means that the yeast is alive and ready to use.

Spiced yeast buns; Almond scones

Simnel Cake

SERVES 12

ALMOND PASTE:
250 g (9 oz) ground almonds
250 g (9 oz) icing sugar, sifted
3 teaspoons lemon juice
1 teaspoon orange flower
    water
few drops almond essence
3 egg yolks

CAKE MIXTURE:
200 g (7 oz) butter
200 g (7 oz) caster sugar
350 g (12 oz) plain flour
pinch of salt
1½ level teaspoons baking
    powder
350 g (12 oz) mixed dried fruit
4 eggs, beaten
milk, if required

DECORATION:
25 g (1 oz) icing sugar
miniature Easter eggs

PREPARATION TIME: *1 hour*

COOKING TIME: *2½ hours*

OVEN: *180°C, 350°F, Gas Mark 4;*
160°C, 325°F, Gas Mark 3

1. To make the almond paste, place the ground almonds and icing sugar in a large mixing bowl and stir well.
2. Make a well in the centre, and add the lemon juice, orange flower water, almond essence and egg yolks.
3. Gradually incorporate this mixture until it forms a dough, then turn on to a pastry board or marble slab dusted with icing sugar, and knead gently until smooth.
4. Divide the paste into 2 balls, one roughly a third of the mixture, the other two-thirds and allow them to relax in the refrigerator until needed.
5. Line a 20 cm (8 inch) loose-based cake tin with greaseproof paper and set aside.
6. Cream the butter and sugar together until light and fluffy.
7. Combine the flour, salt

and baking powder, then mix a little of the flour with the fruit, and stir to make sure the fruit is separated.
8. Beat the eggs slowly into the creamed mixture, adding a little flour from time to time if the mixture appears to be curdling, then stir in the remaining flour and fruit. Add a little milk if necessary to make a heavy dropping consistency.
9. Place half the cake mixture into the prepared tin, then roll out the smaller piece of almond paste to fit exactly over the cake mixture. Cover with the remaining cake mixture and bake in a preheated oven for 45 minutes, then reduce the heat and continue baking for another 1½-1¾ hours.
10. Allow the cake to cool in the tin, then turn on to a wire tray and leave until completely cold.
11. To decorate the cake,

roll out half the remaining almond paste and trim to the exact size of the cake, and place on the top.
12. Use the remaining paste to make 11 balls of equal size and place these round the cake. Dredge the top with a little icing sugar and place under a hot grill for 2-3 minutes to allow the sugar to brown lightly.
13. When cool, place the cake on a serving dish or stand. Pile the miniature eggs in the centre or place them around the edge of the dish. A wide yellow ribbon may be tied round the cake to make it look more festive.

NOTE:
Simnel cake is a classic Easter speciality (though originally it belonged to Mid-Lent or Mothering Sunday). The 11 marzipan balls on the top of the cake represent the 12 apostles minus Judas Iscariot.

Rhubarb and Ginger Jam

MAKES 5 LB JAM

1.5 kg (3 lb) rhubarb, cut into
    chunks
1.5 kg (3 lb) preserving sugar
juice of 3 lemons
25 g (1 oz) ginger root, bruised
    and tied in muslin

PREPARATION TIME: *30 minutes,*
plus overnight soaking

COOKING TIME: *1½ hours*

1. Take a large basin, and make layers with the rhubarb and sugar. Add the lemon juice and allow to stand overnight.
2. Next day, place the rhubarb mixture in a preserving pan, and add the ginger root. (It is best to tie the muslin bag loosely to one of the handles of the pan to make it easier to remove.)
3. Bring the mixture gently

to the boil, then raise the heat and boil the jam rapidly until the temperature reaches 104°C, 220°F on the sugar thermometer. (If you do not possess a thermometer, you can test the setting point of the jam by spooning a little of the mixture on to a cold saucer and allowing it to cool. If the setting point has been reached, the surface will quickly set and will wrinkle up when pressed with the forefinger.) Remove the pan from the heat and allow to cool.
4. Remove the ginger root, then spoon the jam into warm sterilized jam jars.
5. When cold, cover and seal in the usual way.
6. Store in a cool place. The jam will keep for up to 6 months if kept cool and properly sealed.

Banana Tea Loaf

SERVES 8-10

225 g (8 oz) self-raising flour
½ teaspoon salt
½ teaspoon mixed spice
100 g (4 oz) butter, cut into
    pieces
50 g (2 oz) mixed peel
50 g (2 oz) currants
50 g (2 oz) walnut halves,
    chopped
450 g (1 lb) bananas, peeled
1 tablespoon runny honey
2 eggs, beaten
softened butter, to serve

PREPARATION TIME: *20 minutes*

COOKING TIME: *1¼ hours*

OVEN: *180°C, 350°F, Gas Mark 4*

This loaf actually improves with keeping. It may be made up to 1 week in advance, then wrapped in cling film and stored in a cool place or be kept in an airtight container.

1. Lightly grease a 1 kg (2 lb) loaf tin and set aside.
2. Sift the flour, salt and spice into a mixing bowl, and rub in the butter until the mixture resembles fine breadcrumbs.
3. Stir in the mixed peel, currants and walnuts.
4. Mash the bananas with the honey, and stir gently into the mixture with the beaten eggs. Blend well.
5. Pour the mixture into the prepared tin, and bake in a preheated oven for 1¼ hours, or until the loaf is well risen. Remove from the oven and allow to cool in the tin for 10 minutes. Turn on to a wire tray to cool.
6. When ready to serve, slice and butter the bread.

Simnel cake; Banana tea loaf;
Rhubarb and ginger jam

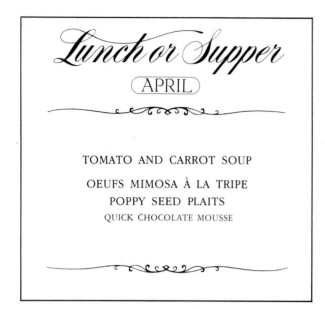

Lunch or Supper

(APRIL)

TOMATO AND CARROT SOUP

OEUFS MIMOSA À LA TRIPE

POPPY SEED PLAITS

QUICK CHOCOLATE MOUSSE

Tomato and Carrot Soup

SERVES 6-8

2 medium onions, peeled and sliced
500 g (1¼ lb) carrots, peeled and diced
25 g (1 oz) butter
3 tablespoons water
750 g (1½ lb) tomatoes, skinned and roughly chopped
2 garlic cloves, peeled and crushed
1 teaspoon caster sugar
2 sprigs fresh or dried thyme
900 ml (1½ pints) chicken stock
1 x 150 ml (5 fl oz) carton double cream
2 egg yolks
salt
freshly ground black pepper

PREPARATION TIME: *30 minutes*

COOKING TIME: *35-45 minutes*

This soup may be prepared in advance and frozen in an airtight plastic container. Do not use a metal container, as it will react against the acid in the tomatoes and discolour the soup. If you find at the last minute you need to serve more than 12, you can add a good quality canned tomato soup.

1. Place the onion and diced carrot in a large saucepan with the butter and water. Place over the heat, and allow the vegetables to soften gently in the butter and water for 10-15 minutes.
2. Add the tomatoes, garlic, sugar, thyme and stock, and bring gently to the boil. Allow to simmer gently for 10-15 minutes.
3. Cool the soup a little, then pass through a liquidizer, food processor or large sieve.
4. Rinse out the pan and pour in the soup. Bring back to the boil and simmer for 5 minutes. Season to taste.
5. Whisk the cream and yolks together. Remove the soup from the heat and add the cream mixture. Check the seasoning. Keep the soup hot until required, but do not allow to boil, otherwise it will curdle.

Oeufs Mimosa à la Tripe

SERVES 6

12 eggs, hard-boiled, shelled and quartered
50 g (2 oz) butter
2 Spanish onions, peeled and thinly sliced
50 g (2 oz) flour
600 ml (1 pint) milk
salt
freshly ground black pepper
2 tablespoons chopped fresh parsley, to garnish

PREPARATION TIME: *20 minutes*

COOKING TIME: *30 minutes*

1. Separate the yolks from the whites of the hard-boiled eggs and pass the yolks through a nylon sieve, using a wooden spoon. Cover the 2 bowls and keep warm while making the sauce.
2. Melt the butter in a saucepan and add the onions. Sweat the onions gently in the butter until soft, but not browned.
3. Stir in the flour and cook the roux for 2-3 minutes. Remove from the heat and gradually stir in the milk.
4. Cook, stirring, until the sauce comes to the boil, then simmer gently for 4-5 minutes. Carefully add salt and pepper.
5. Arrange the quarters of egg white in the base of a gratin dish, then pour over the sauce.
6. Cover completely with the sieved egg yolk, then make a pattern with the parsley to garnish. Serve with Poppy seed plaits (see right).

Poppy Seed Plaits

MAKES 6

450 g (1 lb) strong white flour
1 teaspoon salt
40 g (1½ oz) butter
300 ml (½ pint) tepid milk
15 g (½ oz) fresh yeast
2 tablespoons caster sugar
1 egg, beaten

TO GLAZE:
1 egg
2 tablespoons poppy seeds

PREPARATION TIME: *2 hours, including proving*

COOKING TIME: *15-25 minutes*

OVEN: *200°C, 400°F, Gas Mark 6*

All bread freezes well, so the rolls can be made in advance. Pack them carefully in the freezer, so that they do not get misshapen by heavier packets.

1. Sift the flour and salt into a warm mixing bowl.
2. Melt the butter over a gentle heat in a small pan, then pour on the milk.
3. Place the yeast and sugar in a small bowl, pour on a little of the milk mixture and cream until the yeast has dissolved.
4. Pour the yeast mixture back into the remaining milk, then add the beaten egg and stir well.
5. Make a well in the centre of the flour and pour in the liquid. Beat the flour and liquid together with your hands until a dough is formed.
6. Turn out the dough on to a lightly floured board and knead it for 8-10 minutes until the dough is smooth and no longer sticky.
7. Return the dough to the bowl, then place the bowl in a lightly oiled polythene bag. Set aside in a warm place until the dough has doubled in size.
8. Grease a baking sheet and set aside.
9. Turn the risen dough on to a floured board, punch to deflate the air bubbles and knead gently for 1-2 minutes.
10. Divide the dough into 6 equal sized pieces, and roll each one into a sausage shape. Cut in 3 lengthways, leaving one end just joined together. Plait the 3 pieces over each other, and turn the ends under. Repeat with the other pieces.
11. Place the rolls on the prepared baking sheet and leave to prove in a warm place for 20-30 minutes.
12. Beat the egg for glazing. Brush the rolls with the beaten egg, then sprinkle with poppy seeds.
13. Bake in a preheated oven for 15-25 minutes, or until golden brown. Remove from the oven and allow to cool on a wire tray.

Evening Meal

(APRIL)

ICED CUCUMBER SOUP

PORK CHOPS WITH PICCALILLI

BOILED BUTTERED RED CABBAGE

SAUTÉ POTATOES

MARSHMALLOW PIE

Iced Cucumber Soup

SERVES 6

1 large cucumber, peeled
1 Spanish onion, peeled and
  chopped
600 ml (1 pint) milk
150 ml (¼ pint) chicken stock
salt
freshly ground black pepper
40 g (1½ oz) butter
25 g (1 oz) plain flour
1 teaspoon chopped fresh or
  dried mint
1 x 150 ml (5 fl oz) carton
  single cream

PREPARATION TIME: *20 minutes,
plus cooling*

COOKING TIME: *45 minutes*

It is important to use a good
chicken stock in this recipe
for full flavour.

1. Cut off a quarter of the
cucumber and set aside for
making the garnish.
2. Chop the remaining
cucumber roughly and place
it in a saucepan with the
onion, milk, stock, salt and
pepper.
3. Simmer gently over a low
heat until the vegetables are
soft, about 30 minutes. Cool a
little, then pass through a
liquidizer, food processor or
fine sieve.
4. Rinse out the pan, then
melt the butter and stir in the
flour. Cook the roux over a
gentle heat for 2-3 minutes,
stirring constantly.
5. Remove from the heat and
gradually incorporate the
cucumber liquid, then add
the mint.
6. Return to the heat and
bring gently to the boil,
stirring constantly. Simmer
for 5-6 minutes, then pour
the soup into a large mixing
bowl. Cover with cling film to
prevent a skin forming. Allow
to go cold, then refrigerate
for at least 3 hours.
7. Dice the remaining
cucumber and spread it out
on a plate. Sprinkle with a
little salt and refrigerate. The
salt will draw out the excess
liquid from the diced
cucumber to make it crisp.
8. To serve, whisk the cream
into the soup and pour either
into individual bowls or into
one large tureen. Drain the
excess liquid from the
cucumber and sprinkle a
few pieces on top of each
serving or all of them over
the surface of the tureen.

Pork Chops with Piccalilli

SERVES 6

25 g (1 oz) butter
1 tablespoon oil
6 pork chops
1 onion, peeled and chopped
6 tablespoons piccalilli
1 tablespoon fresh or dried
  marjoram
salt
freshly ground black pepper

PREPARATION TIME: *15 minutes*

COOKING TIME: *45 minutes*

OVEN: *180°C, 350°F, Gas Mark 4*

1. Melt the butter and oil in a
large frying pan and fry the
chops on either side until
lightly browned.
2. Remove the chops from
the pan. Place each one
on a piece of aluminium foil
large enough to wrap loosely
around the chop.
3. Add the onion to the pan
juices, and fry gently for 5
minutes, stirring
occasionally. Divide the
onion between the chops.
4. Place a tablespoon of
piccalilli over the onion, then
sprinkle each one with
marjoram and salt and
pepper.
5. Wrap up each parcel,
making sure that all is well
sealed, then place on a
baking tray and cook in a
preheated oven for 30-35
minutes.
6. To serve, carefully
unwrap each chop, remove
from the foil to a serving dish
and pour over the juices.
Sauté potatoes and boiled,
buttered red cabbage
complement this dish.

Marshmallow Pie

SERVES 6-8

*175 g (6 oz) digestive biscuits,
  crushed*
75 g (3 oz) butter, melted
25 g (1 oz) demerara sugar
15 g (½ oz) gelatine
3 tablespoons water
*225 g (8 oz) pink
  marshmallows*
300 ml (½ pint) milk
75 g (3 oz) chopped walnuts
*1 x 150 ml (5 fl oz) carton
  double cream*

TO DECORATE:
whipped cream
6 maraschino cherries

PREPARATION TIME: *45 minutes,
  plus chilling*

COOKING TIME: *15 minutes*

1. Place the biscuit crumbs
in a bowl, and work in the
melted butter and demerara
sugar.
2. Use this mixture to line
the base and sides of an 18 cm
(7 inch) springform tin. Place
in the refrigerator to set firm
while making the filling.
3. Mix the gelatine with the
water and allow it to melt
over a low heat. Set aside to
cool.
4. Roughly chop the
marshmallows and place
them with the milk in a
saucepan. Heat the mixture
gently, stirring, until the
marshmallows have melted
in the milk. Remove from the
heat, stir in the gelatine and
chopped nuts, and allow the
mixture to cool until it just
begins to set.
5. Whip the cream until it
forms soft peaks and fold it
into the marshmallow
mixture.
6. Pour into the biscuit case
and chill for at least 4 hours.
7. When ready to serve,
remove the pie from the
springform tin and place on a
serving plate.
8. To decorate, place the
cream in a piping bag and
pipe 6 rosettes around the
top of the cake, then place a
maraschino cherry in the
middle of each one.

Margaret Costa's Dinner Party

(APRIL)

SCALLOP AND SWEETCORN SOUP

BRAISED SHOULDER OF LAMB
WITH APRICOT STUFFING

NEW POTATOES

GREEN SALAD

OR

RATATOUILLE EN SALADE

RHUBARB FOOL

Even in the chilliest year, April is touched with the gold of Spring. While you still need to serve a substantial main course, the meal can begin with a lighter soup than usual and the new season's lamb, that is the great treat of this difficult season, gives the promise that Spring is with us already. The vegetables in the ratatouille salad still have a little 'bite' to provide a contrast in texture to the melting and tender braised meat. Forced rhubarb, pink and pretty, makes a delightfully fresh-tasting dessert. Later in the season you may need to increase the grated orange rind to brighten up the colour and taste of the fruit.

Rhubarb fool (recipe page 35)

Scallop and Sweetcorn Soup

SERVES 4

1½ Spanish onions, peeled and
    finely chopped
50 g (2 oz) butter
2 medium potatoes, peeled and
    diced
750 ml (1¼ pints) well
    seasoned chicken stock
salt
freshly ground black pepper
1 small can sweetcorn,
    preferably the softer, creamy
    kind
150 ml (¼ pint) milk
4 scallops
2 egg yolks
about 4 tablespoons double
    cream
chopped chives or fresh parsley
    or chervil

PREPARATION TIME: *20 minutes*

COOKING TIME: *50 minutes*

1. Cook the onions in
the butter till soft and
transparent.
2. Add the potatoes and stir
until all is buttery. Cook very
gently for about 15 minutes.
3. Add the chicken stock and
simmer for about 15 minutes
longer. Put through a
liquidizer or a sieve.
4. Return to the pan and add
plenty of salt and pepper to
taste. Add the drained
sweetcorn kernels and any
flavoursome liquid from the
can and then the milk.
5. Add the scallops chopped
if very large, then stir in the
egg yolks beaten up with the
cream and let the soup slowly
thicken without coming to
boiling point.
6. Scatter as thickly as you
can with chopped green
herbs before serving.
(Chervil is the best if you can
get it.)

Braised Shoulder of Lamb with Apricot Stuffing

SERVES 4

1 boned shoulder new season's
    lamb about 1 kg (2 lb)
    boned weight
salt
freshly ground black pepper
a little oil or melted butter
600 ml (1 pint) chicken stock
175 g (6 oz) diced carrot
175 g (6 oz) diced turnip
175 g (6 oz) diced potato
175 g (6 oz) chopped onion

STUFFING:
25 g (1 oz) butter
1 tablespoon chopped onion
4 rounded tablespoons fresh
    white breadcrumbs
1 teaspoon chopped fresh
    parsley
salt
freshly ground black pepper
1-2 tablespoons milk
75 g (3 oz) dried apricots,
    soaked and coarsely
    chopped

PREPARATION TIME: *45 minutes*

COOKING TIME: *2½ hours*

OVEN: *230°C, 450°F, Gas Mark 8;
    180°C, 350°F, Gas Mark 4*

1. Make the stuffing by
melting the butter and gently
frying the onion in it until
soft, then stirring in the
crumbs, parsley, salt and
pepper. Mix to a soft
consistency with the milk and
add the apricots.
2. Put the boned shoulder of
lamb on the table, cut surface
uppermost, and sprinkle well
with salt and pepper. Spread
the stuffing evenly over the
meat and roll up; secure
firmly with fine string.
3. Brush the joint all over
with oil or melted butter and
place in an open pan in a
preheated oven for 15
minutes to brown.
4. Pour in half the stock and
reduce the heat. Cover and
cook for 45 minutes.
5. Arrange the diced
vegetables round the meat
and add the rest of the stock.
Cover again and cook for
roughly another 1½ hours,
depending on the size of the
joint.
6. Pour off the liquid and
allow it to cool enough for
the fat to rise to the top.
Return the meat and
vegetables to the oven and
cook, uncovered, for another
10 minutes.
7. Meanwhile skim the fat off
the cooking liquid and
reduce it to half by rapid
boiling. Serve this thin gravy
separately, thickened with a
little beurre manié if you like.
8. Serve with new potatoes
and a green salad with a
sharpish French dressing or
with Ratatouille en Salade
(see next page). Alternatively,
if the evening is cold, you
may prefer to serve the
ratatouille hot and it will
complement the meat both
in flavour and appearance
equally well.

Ratatouille en Salade

SERVES 4

about 65 ml (⅛ pint) olive oil
2 large Spanish onions, peeled and chopped
1-2 garlic cloves, peeled and crushed
2 courgettes
2 aubergines, cored and fairly thickly sliced
4 large red peppers, cored and cut in strips
6 good sized tomatoes, quartered
chopped fresh parsley, to garnish

PREPARATION TIME: *30 minutes*

COOKING TIME: *25-30 minutes*

1. Heat the oil in a wide, deep pan and cook the onions and garlic in it for 15 minutes over a low heat.
2. Peel the courgettes in strips to give a pretty striped effect and slice them between 3-5 mm (¼-⅛ inch) thick.
3. Add these to the pan with the sliced aubergines and the peppers. Lastly, add the quartered tomatoes – or use well-drained canned tomatoes – with salt and pepper.
4. Continue cooking gently for not much more than 10 minutes, so as not to lose the texture of the vegetables.
5. Serve garnished with parsley.
6. This dish is intended to be served cold but it can also be gently warmed up if you prefer. Latticed with thin strips of well-drained anchovy fillets, it also makes a delicious hors d'oeuvre.

VARIATION:
You could use 1 x 400 g (14 oz) can tomatoes, well drained and add a little grated lemon rind. The ratatouille also makes a good accompaniment to any chicken or fish dishes, which need a little extra colour.

Rhubarb Fool

SERVES 4

450 g (1 lb) rhubarb, coarsely chopped
50-75 g (2-3 oz) demerara sugar
grated rind of 1 small orange
150-215 ml (5-7½ fl oz) double cream, according to taste
2 small teaspoons Pernod

PREPARATION TIME: *10 minutes*

COOKING TIME: *about 10 minutes*

1. Simmer the rhubarb gently until tender in a very little water with the sugar dissolved in it, and the finely grated orange rind. (Be careful not to overcook it by a second or you will lose its lovely bright colour. Later in the year, you will need more sugar, but now you want to preserve the refreshing tartness of the fruit.)
2. Drain the rhubarb and let it get cold.
3. Stir in the thick cream into which you have already stirred my secret ingredient – the Pernod.
4. Serve, if you can, in old-fashioned custard glasses – or even demi-tasse coffee cups – as it is very rich, with soft sponge fingers or, for a special dinner party, plain chocolate langues de chat or almond tuiles.
(Pictured on page 33.)

Scallop and sweetcorn soup; Braised shoulder of lamb with apricot stuffing; Ratatouille en salade

**GREEN NOODLES WITH
CHICKEN LIVER SAUCE**

**SPRING MIXED SALAD
WITH HONEY DRESSING**

RHUBARB AND ALMOND WHIP

Green Noodles with
Chicken Liver Sauce

SERVES 6

50 g (2 oz) butter
*225 g (8 oz) streaky bacon,
 rinded and roughly chopped*
*1 Spanish onion, peeled and
 chopped*
*1 garlic clove, peeled and
 crushed*
*225 g (8 oz) chicken livers, cut
 into large pieces*
*100 g (4 oz) button
 mushrooms, sliced*
350 g (12 oz) green noodles
1 tablespoon oil

CHEESE SAUCE:
*1 x 300 ml (5 fl oz) carton
 single cream*
150 ml (¼ pint) white wine
3 egg yolks
salt
freshly ground black pepper
*75 g (3 oz) grated Cheddar
 cheese*

TO SERVE:
*1 tablespoon grated Parmesan
 cheese*
*1 tablespoon chopped fresh
 parsley*

PREPARATION TIME: *30 minutes*

COOKING TIME: *35 minutes*

This dish combines an
unusual sauce and colourful
noodles.

1. Melt the butter in a large
frying pan and add the bacon,
onion and garlic. Fry gently
until just soft.
2. Add the chicken livers and
mushrooms and fry, stirring
gently so as not to break up
the livers, until the livers are
cooked.
3. Meanwhile fill a large
saucepan with salted water
and bring to the boil. Add the
noodles and boil gently for
7-8 minutes. Drain well, and
add the oil to the pan, then
return the noodles and toss
well. This will prevent them
from sticking together while
you are finishing the sauce.
Keep warm.
4. To make the cheese
sauce, mix together the
cream, wine, yolks, salt and
pepper in a heavy based
saucepan, and whisk over a
very low heat until the
mixture begins to thicken,
but do not boil. Add the
cheese and stir gently until it
melts.
5. To serve, turn the noodles
on to a serving platter, spoon
over the liver mixture, then
pour over the sauce. Garnish
with Parmesan cheese and
chopped parsley.

Spring Mixed Salad with
Honey Dressing

SERVES 6

*1 curly endive lettuce, washed,
 dried and broken into pieces*
*6 small tomatoes, cut into
 wedges*
*1 bunch of spring onions,
 trimmed and chopped*
*1 bunch radishes, washed and
 sliced*
*2 hard-boiled eggs, peeled and
 chopped*
*1 x 326 g (11½ oz) can
 sweetcorn kernels, drained*

DRESSING:
2 tablespoons runny honey
1 tablespoon lemon juice
1 teaspoon French mustard
2 tablespoons olive oil
salt
freshly ground black pepper

PREPARATION TIME: *30 minutes*

1. Line a large salad bowl
with the curly endive.
2. Arrange the tomato
wedges around the edge of
the bowl. Sprinkle with the
spring onions, radishes and
hard-boiled egg.
3. Reserve 2 tablespoons of
the sweetcorn kernels for the
dressing, then add the
remainder to the salad.
4. To make the dressing,
blend all the ingredients
together in a liquidizer or
food processor, including the
reserved sweetcorn kernels.
5. Pour the dressing over the
salad when ready to serve.

VARIATION:
If a curly endive is not
available, use a crisp Cos
lettuce instead.

Rhubarb and Almond Whip

SERVES 6

*450 g (1 lb) fresh rhubarb, cut
 into 2.5 cm (1 inch) lengths*
3 tablespoons caster sugar
4 tablespoons ground almonds
*1 x 300 ml (10 fl oz) carton
 double or whipping cream*

TO DECORATE:
*1 x 150 ml (5 fl oz) double or
 whipping cream*
6 ratafia biscuits

PREPARATION TIME: *25 minutes,
 plus cooling*

COOKING TIME: *20-25 minutes*

If you are lucky enough to
have rhubarb growing in
your garden, cover the plant
with a box or large bucket as
soon as it shows signs of
growing. The rhubarb will
grow very quickly under
these conditions, and the
stems will be pink and
tender. Many of the farms
where you can 'pick your
own' also use this method.

1. Place the rhubarb in a
large saucepan with the sugar
and as little water as possible
– just enough to half cover
the fruit.
2. Put on the lid and cook
over a gentle heat until the
fruit is tender and just
beginning to break up.
3. Purée the fruit in a
liquidizer or food processor,
or pass it through a sieve.
Leave until cold.
4. Stir in the ground
almonds and check for
sweetness.
5. Whisk the cream until
thick, then fold evenly into
the rhubarb purée. Divide
the mixture between 6
individual glasses and chill
well.
6. When ready to serve,
whip the cream for
decoration and fill into a
forcing bag fitted with a rose
tube. Pipe swirls of cream on
the top of each glass and
decorate each with a ratafia
biscuit.

Evening Meal
MAY

EGG AND CUCUMBER MOUSSE

SAFFRON STUFFED SHOULDER OF LAMB

SPRING CABBAGE

PARSLEYED NEW POTATOES

GLAZED GOOSEBERRY BOATS

Egg and Cucumber Mousse

SERVES 6

½ cucumber
salt
6 cold hard-boiled eggs, peeled
1 x 450 ml (15 fl oz) can jellied
  consommé, very cold
1 x 300 ml (10 fl oz) carton
  double or whipping cream,
  chilled
few drops anchovy essence
freshly ground black pepper

TO GARNISH:
slices of cucumber
100 g (¼ lb) peeled prawns
1 tablespoon chopped fresh
  parsley

PREPARATION TIME: *20 minutes,*
  plus chilling

COOKING TIME: *15 minutes*

The secret of making this recipe is to have all the ingredients completely cold before preparation, as the jellied consommé works as a setting agent.

1. Peel and dice the cucumber. Spread out the pieces on a plate, and sprinkle with salt. Leave in the refrigerator for at least 1 hour to draw off the excess water. Drain off the water when ready for use.
2. Place 3 eggs and half the consommé in a liquidizer or food processor and purée together. Turn into a bowl, and repeat the process with the remaining eggs and consommé.
3. Whip the cream until stiff, then fold into the egg and consommé mixture together with the cucumber, anchovy essence and add a little salt and freshly ground black pepper, according to taste. Pour this mixture into a soufflé dish and chill until set.
4. Before serving, garnish the mousse by making a ring of overlapping cucumber slices round the edge of the dish. Arrange the prawns attractively in the centre and sprinkle with chopped parsley.

Saffron Stuffed Shoulder of Lamb

SERVES 6

300 ml (1/2 pint) water, salted
10 strands of saffron
40 g (11/2 oz) long grain rice
25 g (1 oz) butter
1 medium onion, peeled and
  finely chopped
6 prunes, soaked overnight,
  stoned and chopped
50 g (2 oz) walnut halves,
  chopped
1 teaspoon chopped fresh or
  dried mint
1 egg, beaten
salt
freshly ground black pepper
1 x 1.75 g (4 lb) shoulder of
  lamb, boned
2 garlic cloves, peeled and
  sliced lengthways
2 tablespoons plain flour
75 g (3 oz) butter, softened
300 ml (1/2 pint) stock
150 ml (1/4 pint) wine

PREPARATION TIME: *40 minutes,
  plus soaking*

COOKING TIME: *2 1/2 hours*

OVEN: *180°C, 350°F, Gas Mark 4*

Many people avoid buying
shoulders of lamb because
they can be very fatty, but if
you buy English lamb during
April and May, the animals
are so young that the layers of
fat have not yet had a chance
to develop, and the young
meat is deliciously sweet and
tender. Your butcher will
bone the meat for you,
leaving a natural pocket for
the stuffing when removing
the blade bone. The bones
may be boiled up with
onions, carrots and herbs to
make the stock for the sauce,
rather than using a stock
cube.

1. Place the salted water and
the saffron strands in a
pan and bring to the boil.
2. Add the rice, and simmer
over a gentle heat for 15-20
minutes, until all the water
has evaporated and the rice is
cooked through.
3. Meanwhile, melt the
butter in a small pan and
cook the onion gently until it
becomes translucent. Do not
allow it to brown.
4. Stir in the prunes, walnuts
and mint, then add this
mixture to the saffron rice,
bind with the beaten egg and
add salt and pepper to taste.
5. Stuff the joint with the
mixture, then roll up and
secure with butcher's string
at 5 cm (2 inch) intervals.
6. Make diagonal slits in the
skin on the top of the joint,
and slip a piece of garlic into
each one.
7. Place the plain flour in
one end of the roasting tin
and put in the meat with one
of its cut edges resting on the
flour. This will allow the flour
to soak up the meat juices
during cooking, thus both
thickening and giving extra
flavour to the gravy.
8. Smear the butter over the
joint, and place in a
preheated oven for 2 hours,
basting occasionally.
9. Remove the meat to a
serving platter and keep
warm. Pour off two-thirds of
the fat into a small bowl, then
place the roasting tin over a
low heat.
10. Stir well with a flat spoon
to incorporate the flour and
the fat, and allow to cook for
2-3 minutes. Pour on the
stock and wine, and gently
bring to the boil. Simmer for
5 minutes, add salt and
pepper, then strain and serve
in a sauceboat with the meat.
Serve with spring cabbage
and new potatoes, tossed in
butter and sprinkled with
chopped fresh parsley.

Glazed Gooseberry Boats

SERVES 6

1 quantity of sweet pastry (see Citrus Flan, page 18)

FILLING:

225 g (8 oz) gooseberries, topped and tailed

75 g (3 oz) sugar

4 tablespoons water

GLAZE:

4 tablespoons apricot jam, sieved

2 tablespoons water

1 x 150 ml (5 fl oz) carton double or whipping cream, whipped, to decorate

PREPARATION TIME: *40 minutes, plus cooling*

COOKING TIME: *45 minutes*

OVEN: *180°C, 350°F, Gas Mark 4*
150°C, 300°F, Gas Mark 2

1. To make the boats, roll out the pastry and use it to line 12 boat-shaped pastry moulds.
2. Prick the bases of the pastry and bake in a preheated oven for 8-10 minutes, or until the pastry is crisp, and golden brown around the edges.
3. Remove the pastry boats from the tins, and allow them to cool on a wire tray.
4. Place the gooseberries in an ovenproof dish, sprinkle with the sugar, then pour over the water. Cook in a preheated cool oven until the fruit is just tender. The cooking time depends on the ripeness of the gooseberries, but remove them from the oven before they begin to break up. Allow to cool in the dish.
5. When the gooseberries are quite cold, fill them into the pastry boats and prepare the glaze.
6. Place the apricot jam and water in a small saucepan and allow to melt over a gentle heat. Bring to simmering point and cook for 2-3 minutes. Using a pastry brush, glaze each pastry boat.
7. For the decoration, fill the whipped cream into a forcing bag fitted with a small rose tube, and pipe each boat with a shell pattern.

NOTE:

The good old English gardeners always say that gooseberries are ready to pick at Whitsuntide, but, as this is a movable feast, no-one quite knows how they work this saying out! However the main crop comes during May, and if you are fond of the fruit, they are well worth freezing, as they are not popular enough to be grown abroad for export, and the season in this country is relatively short.

Dinner Party

MAY

ASPARAGUS WITH
GREEN MAYONNAISE

MELBA TOAST

CALVES' LIVER WITH SAGE SAUCE

BABY BROAD BEANS

POMMES DE TERRE FORESTIÈRE

PRALINE CHARLOTTE

Asparagus with Green Mayonnaise

SERVES 6

2 bundles asparagus

GREEN MAYONNAISE:
3 egg yolks
1 tablespoon finely chopped
*   chives*
1 tablespoon finely chopped
*   fresh parsley*
1 tablespoon lemon juice
300 ml (½ pint) olive oil
salt
freshly ground black pepper

PREPARATION TIME: *30 minutes,*
*   plus cooling*

COOKING TIME: *20-25 minutes*

Making mayonnaise in the liquidizer or food processor saves a great deal of time, but if you have to prepare it by hand the oil must be added much more slowly, beating well between each addition to save curdling. If the mixture does begin to curdle, it is possible to bring it back by whisking in a teaspoon of very cold water.

1. Wash the asparagus and trim the ends. Scrape the lower half of each spear, then divide into 6 bundles.
2. Tie each bunch firmly, finishing with a long-ended bow. (This makes it easier to remove the string after cooking.)
3. Fill a large pan with salted water and bring to the boil. If you have a pan deep enough for the spears to stand upright, so much the better, and the tender points can then be above the water level. This means that they are steamed while the firmer parts of the stalks are actually cooking in the water.
4. Place the lid on the pan, and boil until just tender. Do not overcook.
5. Carefully remove the bundles and place them on a wire tray to drain and go cold.
6. To make the sauce, place the yolks, herbs and lemon juice in a liquidizer or food processor and mix for 1-2 minutes. Keeping the motor running, pour in the oil in a very thin stream until all is incorporated. Add salt and pepper.
7. To serve, untie the bundles of asparagus and place 1 bundle on each plate. Serve the sauce separately and accompany the dish with Melba toast (see this page).

Melba Toast

Melba toast is extremely simple to make, and stores well in a sealed container for up to a week so you can save time by making several batches at a time.

As an accompaniment to the asparagus, take 6 slices of medium sliced bread and toast it on either side. While still hot, cut off the crusts and place the flat of your hand on the remaining toast. Now slice the toast in half horizontally carefully. Place the untoasted sides under a hot grill, making sure that the shelf is not too high, as the melba toasts will curl up. Watch the grill all the time at this stage, as the thin toasts brown extremely quickly. Serve warm or cold.

Calves' Liver with Sage Sauce

SERVES 6

75 g (3 oz) butter
1 tablespoon oil
6 slices calves' liver, 90-100 g
  (3½-4 oz) each in weight
1 medium onion, peeled and
  chopped
75 g (3 oz) button mushrooms,
  sliced
1 tablespoon plain flour
300 ml (½ pint) beef stock
150 ml (¼ pint) red wine
1 tablespoon chopped fresh or
  dried sage
salt
freshly ground black pepper
sprigs of fresh sage leaves, to
  garnish

PREPARATION TIME: *20 minutes*

COOKING TIME: *20 minutes*

The secret of cooking calves'
liver is to have it very thinly
sliced, and your butcher will
do this for you to save cut
fingers!

1. Heat the butter and oil in a
large heavy frying pan, and
fry the liver quickly on either
side until it is light golden
brown. Remove from the pan
and keep warm.
2. Cook the onion in the pan
juices for 3-4 minutes, then
add the mushrooms and
cook for a further 3-4
minutes. Remove the pan
from the heat.
3. Sprinkle in the flour and
mix gently, taking care not to
break up the mushrooms.
4. Return the pan to the heat
and gradually incorporate
the stock and wine. Add the
sage, salt and pepper.
5. Return the liver to the pan
and coat with the sauce.
Simmer gently for 8-10
minutes.
6. To serve, arrange the liver
slices overlapping on a
serving dish, pour over the
sauce and garnish with the
fresh sage leaves. Serve with
Pommes de terre forestière
(see below) and buttered
baby broad beans.

Pommes de Terre Forestière

SERVES 6

680 g (1½ lb) old potatoes,
  peeled and cut into 1 cm
  (½ inch) dice
25 g (1 oz) butter
2 tablespoons oil
50 g (2 oz) bacon, rinded and
  roughly chopped
1 medium onion, peeled and
  finely chopped
75 g (3 oz) small button
  mushrooms, sliced
2 tablespoons chopped fresh
  parsley
salt
freshly ground black pepper

PREPARATION TIME: *20 minutes*

COOKING TIME: *30 minutes*

Bacon, onion and
mushrooms add interest to
these sautéed potatoes.

1. Blanch the diced potato in
boiling salted water for 3-4
minutes. Drain and allow to
dry in the colander.
2. Melt the butter and oil
together in a large heavy
frying pan and add the bacon
and onion. Cook, stirring,
until light golden brown.
3. Add the mushrooms and
potatoes and fry until all is
mixed and gently browned.
Stir very gently during the
cooking period to prevent
the ingredients from
breaking up.
4. Stir in the parsley, salt and
pepper. Turn into a serving
dish.
5. If you wish to keep the
potatoes warm for any length
of time, cover with a butter
paper or a piece of
aluminium foil.

Praline Charlotte

SERVES 6

100 g (4 oz) almonds in their skins
100 g (4 oz) caster sugar

CHARLOTTE:
3 egg yolks
75 g (3 oz) caster sugar
250 ml (8 fl oz) milk
15 g (½ oz) powdered gelatine, melted in 2 tablespoons water
250 ml (8 fl oz) double cream
1 packet sponge finger biscuits, roughly broken
1 x 150 ml (5 fl oz) carton double or whipping cream, whipped

PREPARATION TIME: *1¼ hours*

COOKING TIME: *40 minutes, plus chilling*

Praline may be made in advance and stored in a screwtopped jar or sealed polythene bag in a dry cupboard. The finished pudding may also be wrapped and frozen in its mould for up to 4 weeks. Allow at least 3 hours for defrosting before turning out and decorating.

1. To make the praline, place the almonds and sugar together in a saucepan and heat gently, stirring occasionally, until the sugar has melted. Raise the heat, and boil, without stirring, until a rich caramel is obtained.
2. Pour the mixture on to an oiled baking sheet and set aside until quite cold. Break up into small pieces, then grind to a rough powder in a coffee grinder or liquidizer.
3. To make the charlotte, line the base of a 15 cm (6 inch) charlotte mould with oiled greaseproof paper. If you do not possess a proper mould, a 15 cm (6 inch) cake tin will suffice.
4. Cream the yolks and sugar together until thick and pale in colour.
5. Heat the milk until almost simmering, then pour it on to the egg mixture and stir well. Strain into a double boiler or cast iron saucepan, and cook very slowly, without boiling, and stirring gently, until the custard thickens enough to coat the back of a wooden spoon.
6. Remove from the heat and add the softened gelatine and the praline. Pour into a large mixing bowl and leave in a cool place, stirring occasionally, until the mixture is just beginning to set around the sides of the bowl.
7. Lightly whisk the cream and fold into the custard.
8. Place the prepared charlotte mould in a large bowl containing roughly crushed ice cubes.
9. Pour a layer of the custard into the base, then cover with a layer of the biscuits. When the first layer has set, pour in another layer of the custard. Continue until the mould is full. You may have to work quite quickly as the crushed ice causes the custard to set almost immediately.
10. Cover with cling film and chill for at least 2 hours before turning out. To unmould, dip the tin in very hot water for a few seconds, then turn out on to a serving plate. Decorate with rosettes of whipped cream.

Buffet Party
MAY

FRESH SALMON PÂTÉ

LAYERED FILLET OF PORK TERRINE
WITH GARLIC BREAD

CHICKEN AND HORSERADISH
MAYONNAISE

MELON, WALNUT AND AVOCADO SALAD

GREEN SALAD WITH
THREE CHEESE DRESSING

TOMATO SALAD FROM PROVENCE

CHOCOLATE & PISTACHIO GÂTEAU

CITRUS SYLLABUB

HOW TO DRESS A PINEAPPLE
AS CENTREPIECE

Careful organization will reduce the complications of preparing this meal. The Fresh salmon pâté will keep in the refrigerator without its decoration for at least 3 days. The flavour is delicate, so make sure it is really well covered in cling film to keep out the flavours of the other contents of your refrigerator. The terrine and the garlic butter may be made up and stored in the freezer, and the chickens may be cooked, shredded and stored in the freezer also. Pack the shredded chicken in heavy duty freezer bags, making sure that the bags are well sealed.

The salad dressings may be made up the day before and stored in screw-topped glass jars, whereas the gâteau may be made in advance and frozen in an airtight plastic container.

BACK LEFT TO RIGHT:
Chicken and horseradish mayonnaise (recipe page 47); Pineapple centrepiece (see page 49); Green salad with three cheese dressing (recipe page 48). FRONT LEFT TO RIGHT: *Layered fillet of pork terrine (recipe page 46); Tomato salad from Provence (recipe page 48)*

Fresh Salmon Pâté

SERVES 12

750 g (1½ lb) fresh salmon or
*   sea-trout*
1 small onion, peeled and
*   sliced*
1 carrot, peeled and sliced
2 bay leaves
150 ml (¼ pint) white wine
175 g (6 oz) unsalted butter,
*   creamed*

SAUCE:

75 g (3 oz) butter
75 g (3 oz) flour
600 ml (1 pint) milk
2 teaspoons lemon juice
salt
freshly ground black pepper

TO GARNISH:

½ cucumber, cut into thin
*   rings*
1 hard-boiled egg, yolk sieved,
*   white chopped*
1 tablespoon chopped fresh
*   parsley*

PREPARATION TIME: *40 minutes,*
*   plus cooling*

COOKING TIME: *40 minutes*

If making this pâté in
advance, do not garnish until
ready to serve. Fresh salmon
is available from December
to August, whereas sea-trout
is at its best during the
summer.

Garlic Bread

SERVES 12

2 French loaves
350 g (12 oz) butter, softened
6 garlic cloves, peeled and
*   crushed*
salt
freshly ground black pepper
2 teaspoons French seed
*   mustard*

PREPARATION TIME: *20 minutes*

COOKING TIME: *15 minutes*

OVEN: *200°C, 400°F, Gas Mark 6*

1. Place the salmon in a large
saucepan and add the onion,
carrot, bay leaves and wine.
Add just enough water to
cover, then bring the fish
slowly to the boil. Simmer
gently for 15-20 minutes,
then remove from the heat
and allow the fish to cool in
the liquid.
2. Meanwhile make up the
sauce base. Melt the butter in
a saucepan, remove from the
heat and stir in the flour.
Cook the roux for 2-3
minutes, then gradually add
the milk, beating well
between each addition until
really smooth. Simmer gently
for 3-4 minutes, add the
lemon juice, salt and pepper
and allow to cool.
3. Skin and flake the cooked
salmon, and pass it through a
food processor or pound it
with a pestle and mortar.
4. When all the ingredients
are cool, blend together the
fish, sauce and creamed
butter. Check the seasoning
and place the pâté in a dish.
Cover with clingfilm until
ready to garnish.
5. Arrange the cucumber
round the outside, then the
chopped egg white and finish
with the sieved egg yolk and
chopped parsley.

1. Cut each loaf in 2.5 cm
(1 inch) slices – not quite
through the base of the loaf,
but leaving it just joined.
2. Cream the butter in a
mixing bowl and add the
garlic, salt, pepper and
mustard.
3. Spread a little of the butter
mixture between each slice
of bread, re-form the loaf and
wrap loosely in foil.
4. Place in a preheated oven
and bake for 15 minutes.
5. Unwrap the loaf and serve
immediately with the Layered
fillet of pork terrine.

Layered Fillet of Pork Terrine

SERVES 12

3 bay leaves
5 juniper berries or black
*   peppercorns*
200 g (7 oz) streaky bacon
350 g (12 oz) pig's liver
1 small onion, peeled
1 garlic clove, peeled
350 g (12 oz) sausage meat
1 teaspoon mixed herbs
2 hard-boiled eggs, finely
*   chopped*
salt
freshly ground black pepper
350 g (12 oz) pork tenderloin

PREPARATION TIME: *40 minutes*

COOKING TIME: *1½ hours*

OVEN: *180°C, 350°F, Gas Mark 4*

If you do not possess a
proper earthenware or
cast-iron terrine dish, this
mixture will fill a 1 kg (2 lb)
loaf tin. Terrines are best
made at least 1 day in
advance, so that they can be
weighted over night, but they
store well, and can be kept in
the refrigerator for up to 4
days as long as they are
properly wrapped to retain
the moisture.

1. Lightly grease a 1 kg (2 lb)
loaf tin, or a terrine of
comparable size. Make a
pattern on the base with
upturned bay leaves and
juniper berries or
peppercorns.
2. Line the terrine with
streaky bacon. Do not trim
any overlapping pieces, as
they can be folded over to
help keep the filling in place.
3. Mince together the liver,
onion and garlic, then mix
well with the sausage meat,
herbs, hard-boiled egg, salt
and pepper.
4. Slice the pork tenderloin
lengthways into thin strips.
Place these strips between 2
sheets of greaseproof paper
and beat them with a rolling

pin until thin and tenderized.
5. Place a layer of the liver
mixture in the base of the
terrine, then cover this with
pork fillet, and repeat these
layers until the dish is full.
Fold over any overlapping
bacon.
6. Place the lid on the
terrine, or, if using a loaf tin,
seal well with foil. Cook the
terrine in a bain-marie (a pan
filled with water to halfway
up the sides of the dish) in a
preheated oven for 1½
hours.
7. Remove the lid from the
terrine, cover with
greaseproof paper and place
heavyweights or a clean brick
on the top to press the terrine
into a good shape. Cool, then
refrigerate.
8. When ready to serve,
uncover and turn out the
terrine on to a serving platter.
Carve into slices as required.
Garlic Bread (see left) makes
a pleasant accompaniment.
(Pictured on page 44.)

Melon, walnut and avocado salad; Fresh salmon pâté with Garlic bread

Melon, Walnut and Avocado Salad

SERVES 12

1 honeydew melon
2 avocado pears
1 lettuce, washed and shredded
50 g (2 oz) walnut halves,
  chopped
25 g (1 oz) sultanas

DRESSING:

150 ml (5 fl oz) olive oil
50 ml (2 fl oz) red wine vinegar
juice of ⅛ lemon
1 teaspoon French whole seed
  mustard
1 teaspoon sugar
1 teaspoon dried dill weed
salt
freshly ground black pepper

PREPARATION TIME: *30 minutes*

When choosing the melon and avocados, select fruits that are just ripe, but still firm, otherwise they will break up during the preparation of the salad. If making the salad in advance, cover with clingfilm to prevent discoloration.

1. Split the melon in half lengthways, remove the seeds and cut out rounds of flesh with a ball cutter. If you do not have such a cutter, dice the melon flesh into 1cm (½ inch) cubes.
2. Halve each avocado and discard the stone. Remove the peel and dice the flesh. Add to the melon balls and toss together.
3. Arrange the shredded lettuce in a shallow salad bowl, then spoon over the melon and avocado. Sprinkle the walnuts and sultanas over the top.
4. To make the dressing, place all the ingredients in a screw-top jar and shake vigorously until well-blended. Taste and adjust the seasoning. Pour over the salad and serve.

Chicken and Horseradish Mayonnaise

SERVES 12

2 x 1.5 kg (3½ lb) chickens,
  poached, cooled and
  shredded
450 g (1 lb) waxy potatoes,
  cooked, peeled and sliced
225 g (8 oz) button
  mushrooms, sliced
3 tablespoons chopped fresh
  parsley
3 tablespoons horseradish
  sauce
600 ml (1 pint) mayonnaise
salt
freshly ground black pepper

DECORATION:

3 hard-boiled eggs
175 g (6 oz) peeled prawns
1 tablespoon chopped fresh
  parsley

PREPARATION TIME: *40 minutes,*
  plus cooling

COOKING TIME: *1 hour 20*
  minutes for poaching the
  chickens

1. Place the shredded chicken in a large mixing bowl together with the potato slices, button mushrooms and chopped parsley.
2. Mix the horseradish into the mayonnaise and add salt and pepper.
3. Pour the mixture over the chicken, and toss gently together with the fingertips or 2 large forks. When all is incorporated, check the seasoning, then pile the mixture on to a large serving platter.
4. To decorate the dish, separate the eggs, chop the whites finely and sieve the yolks. Sprinkle the whites over the chicken. Make a pattern over the top of the dish with the sieved yolks, peeled prawns and chopped parsley.
(Pictured on page 44.)

NOTE:
The chickens can be poached and stripped in advance, and kept in the refrigerator for 1-2 days or deep-frozen for up to 4 weeks. To get plenty of flavour into the chicken flesh, season the poaching liquid and add a little onion and carrot, and a bouquet garni. The flesh will be more moist if you have time to allow the chickens to cool in the cooking liquid before stripping the carcasses.

Green Salad with Three Cheese Dressing

SERVES 12

1 bunch of spring onions, trimmed and sliced lengthways

1/2 cucumber, sliced into thin rings

1 lettuce, washed, dried, and broken into pieces

4 small courgettes, cut into matchstick lengths

1 box cress, cut and washed

1 tablespoon chopped chives

DRESSING:

100 g (4 oz) Stilton cheese

100 g (4 oz) cream cheese

75 g (3 oz) Camembert

1 tablespoon runny honey

1 tablespoon lemon juice

3 tablespoons olive oil

1 teaspoon French seed mustard

salt

freshly ground black pepper

PREPARATION TIME: *30 minutes*

1. Place all the prepared salad ingredients in a large salad bowl.
2. Place all the dressing ingredients in a liquidizer or food processor, and blend until all is really well incorporated.
3. Pour the dressing over the salad and toss well.
(Pictured on page 45.)

VARIATION:

Other cheeses may be used in place of those in the recipe but make sure that you use one blue cheese, one cream cheese and one strong, creamy French cheese.

Tomato Salad from Provence

SERVES 12

6 continental tomatoes, skinned and sliced

1 Spanish onion, peeled and cut into rings

1 tablespoon basil, fresh or dried, chopped

DRESSING:

2 tablespoons olive oil

1 tablespoon white wine vinegar

1 teaspoon fresh mustard

1 garlic clove, peeled and crushed

2 teaspoons lemon juice

salt

freshly ground black pepper

PREPARATION TIME: *30 minutes, plus standing*

1. Arrange the tomato and onion slices in layers in a shallow dish, sprinkling with a little basil between each layer. Finish with a layer of onion.
2. To make the dressing, mix all the ingredients together and place them in a blender or food processor. If you do not possess either of these machines, place all the ingredients in a screw-top jar and shake really well.
3. Pour the dressing over the salad at least 30 minutes before serving.
(Pictured on page 45.)

The 'nobbly' continental tomatoes are imported nearly all the year round, but if they are unavailable, use large ordinary tomatoes.

Chocolate and Pistachio Gâteau

SERVES 8-10

SPONGE:

4 eggs

120 g (4 1/2 oz) caster sugar

100 g (4 oz) plain flour, sifted

40 g (1 1/2 oz) butter, melted and cooled

BUTTER ICING:

65 g (2 1/2 oz) caster sugar

150 ml (1/4 pint) water

2 egg yolks, beaten

150 g (5 oz) unsalted butter, slightly softened

2 tablespoons ground pistachio nuts

a little green colouring

50 g (2 oz) chocolate, melted and cooled

DECORATION:

100 g (4 oz) blanched almonds, chopped and toasted

50 g (2 oz) whole pistachio nuts, split in half

PREPARATION TIME: *40-50 minutes, plus cooling*

COOKING TIME: *35-40 minutes*

OVEN: *180°C, 350°F, Gas Mark 4*

If making in advance and freezing, defrost this gâteau for at least 3 hours before using. The butter icing has a tendency to melt in the piping bag due to heat from your hands, so work quickly, then chill or freeze straightaway.

1. To make the sponge, place the eggs and sugar in the bowl of an electric mixer and whisk at high speed until the mixture becomes thick and mousse-like.
2. Remove the bowl from the machine, and gently fold in the flour and butter until all is well incorporated.
3. Pour the cake mixture into a greased 20 cm (8 inch) cake tin and bake in a preheated oven for 35-40 minutes, or until the cake is firm to the touch and begins to shrink from the sides of the tin. Turn the cake on to a wire tray to cool.
4. Meanwhile, make the butter icing. Place the sugar and water in a saucepan and allow the sugar to dissolve over a gentle heat. Raise the heat and boil to the soft thread stage (107°C, 225°F, on a sugar thermometer or when the syrup will form a fine, thin thread if allowed to fall from a spoon on to a dish). The syrup should not begin to colour at this stage.
5. Cool a little, then pour it very slowly on to the beaten yolks, whisking all the time. Continue whisking the mixture until it is cool, thick and fluffy.
6. Beat in the butter, a nut at a time, until all is incorporated.
7. Set aside one-third of the butter icing and stir in the ground pistachio nuts, adding a few drops of green colouring. Flavour the remaining icing by gently stirring in the melted chocolate.
8. When the cake is completely cold, split it in half and sandwich together with a little of the chocolate icing. Spread the side of the cake with more of the chocolate icing and coat with the chopped almonds.
9. Take 2 icing bags fitted with small rose tubes and fill 1 with the remaining chocolate icing and the other with pistachio icing.
10. Pipe 2 opposite quarters of the cake with 1 flavour, and the other 2 quarters with the other flavour. Decorate the top with the pistachio nuts.

Pineapple as a Centrepiece

1. Choose a large ripe pineapple with good leaves. The best variety to buy is called a Hass, which is available in May. It has large and attractive leaves and a wonderful flavour.
2. Cut off the top and base. Discard the base and set the leafy top aside.
3. Stand the pineapple upright and, using a large sharp knife, cut away the skin quite deeply. Remove any of the pitted part of the skin that remains.
4. Turn the pineapple on to its side and slice thinly, then re-form the fruit slices in the order in which they were cut.
5. Stand the pineapple upright on a serving dish and pour a little Kirsch or another liqueur of your choice over the fruit. Replace the top leafy slice. The base of the pineapple may be decorated with fresh fruits or decorative leaves from the garden. (Pictured on page 45.)

Citrus Syllabub

SERVES 8

24 ratafia biscuits
50 g (2 oz) caster sugar
rind of 1 orange
rind of 1 lemon
juice of ½ orange
juice of ½ lemon
pinch of cinnamon
125 ml (¼ pint) sherry
600 ml (20 fl oz) single cream

PREPARATION TIME: *20 minutes, plus chilling*

This recipe is a light, fresh alternative for those who do not wish for the richness of the chocolate pistachio gâteau. Do not prepare more than 3 hours in advance. It is quickly made provided you have an electric mixer.

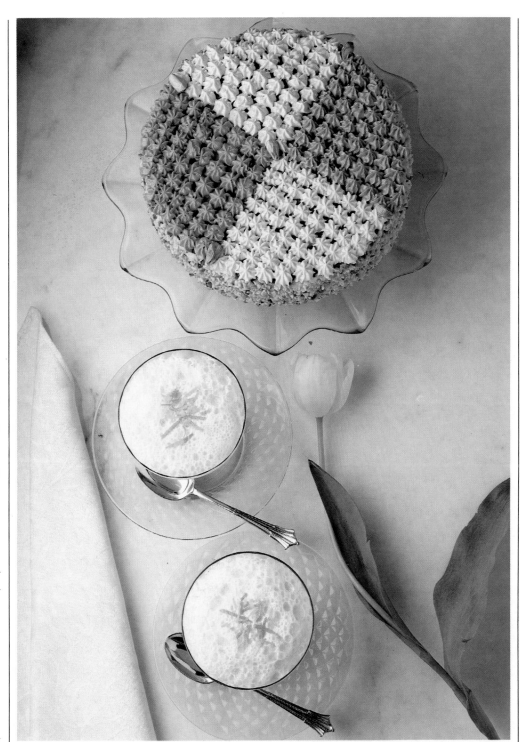

Chocolate and pistachio gâteau; Citrus syllabub

1. Arrange 3 ratafia biscuits in the bases of 8 coupe glasses or saucer champagne glasses.
2. Take a large mixing bowl and put in the sugar, half the orange and lemon rind, all the fruit juice, a pinch of cinnamon and the sherry. Stir until the sugar has dissolved.
3. Pour in the cream and whisk, preferably with an electric mixer.
4. As the froth forms, scoop it off and spoon it over the ratafias.
5. Keep whisking and removing the froth until all the mixture is used up, then chill the glasses in the refrigerator.
6. When ready to serve, sprinkle each one with the reserved grated lemon and orange rind. They could be accompanied by light sponge fingers, if desired.

Summer

Long days, balmy evenings and short nights. Summer has arrived and with it the wonderful array of new vegetables, salads, soft fruits and herbs to make the lighter meals that we associate with summer. This is also the season for jam-making and for storing up home-grown herbs for the winter.

VEGETABLES

Although new potatoes, imported from abroad, will have been with us since March, June sees the start of the English new potatoes. Baby new potatoes are delicious just scrubbed, boiled and served with melted butter and sea salt. The other young vegetables are now arriving in the shops. Broad beans when very small can be boiled in the pods and eaten whole, as can the new peas, but look out for 'Mange tout', a variety of pea that is grown to be eaten pods and all.

Home-produced tomatoes, cucumbers and radishes are now plentiful and if you have a glut of lettuces, cucumbers and tomatoes in the garden, all can be turned into light soups to be served hot or chilled.

The vegetables that are in the shops now, such as runner beans and young carrots, need very little cooking. Simmer them in the minimum of slightly salted water until they still have a little 'bite' and this way all the goodness is preserved.

Most people regard salads as the perfect summer meal and the variety of ingredients available is endless. Many larger supermarkets and greengrocers can now offer many different kinds of lettuce, as well as the usual cabbage lettuce, Cos and Webb's Wonder. Look out for Iceberg, a round, tight lettuce which has very crunchy leaves and keeps very well, besides the more unusual imported varieties such as the curly-leaved endive and the Italian red-leaved lettuce known as radiccio.

A good dressing can lift any salad right out of the ordinary. You can experiment with the classic French dressing by the addition of fresh herbs or ingredients like honey or whole-grain mustard.

FRUIT

Soft fruits now appear and it is worth looking out for farms where raspberries, strawberries, red and black currants can be picked in bulk at very reasonable prices for freezing and jam-making. Raspberries and currants are best 'open frozen' in the freezer on foil-lined trays, as this keeps them whole and separate. They can then be transferred to bags or rigid containers. Although strawberries can be frozen by this method, they do lose their firmness when thawed, so are better frozen as a purée.

Do not think of summer fruits as just a sweet course. Strawberries and sliced cucumber in a French dressing make a very refreshing summer starter or side salad dish and peaches and apricots seem to have an affinity with cream cheese to serve as a starter or salad.

In summer fresh fruit, however, is the natural dessert, either on its own or with some cream or yogurt. Do consider turning some of the fruit into ice creams and sorbets, which are very welcome on hot summer days, and can be the basis of many summer desserts. A very simple method of making ice cream is shown on page 54.

HERBS

Fresh herbs enhance so many dishes and should be used as much as possible. By adding some of these you can bring out the flavour of foods and lift some dishes into a class of their own – a simple tomato salad is transformed by the addition of some chopped fresh basil, for instance. Specific herbs have long been associated with certain foods; for example, rosemary as well as mint with lamb, sage with pork, tarragon with chicken. Try grilling fish over some fennel or dill.

Most herbs can be preserved by freezing or drying. To freeze, just wash and dry, put the leaves into polythene bags and freeze; or they can be chopped, mixed with a little water and frozen in ice cube trays.

To dry herbs, it is essential that they are put into a dry place, and then either quick-dried by spreading on newspaper and putting in a warm place like an airing cupboard, where they are usually dried in about twenty-four hours, or by drying in the open air. Tied into bunches and hung upside down in a cool, dry, airy place, the herbs will take about two to three weeks to dry. When quite dry crumble them and store in airtight jars. Remember that the flavour of herbs is much more concentrated when dried, so only about half the amount of dried herb is necessary compared with the fresh one.

PICNICS AND BARBECUES

One of the great pleasures of summer is eating in the open air, at a picnic or barbecue. When planning a picnic, choose food that will travel well. Take salads that can be dressed in advance, like a rice salad. Pâtés, raised pies and flans are ideal picnic food, as are egg dishes such as Scotch eggs, and a thick Spanish omelette is just as delicious served cold as hot. Don't bother too much about puddings for a picnic, although a cake is always acceptable, served with some easily transportable fruit such as peaches and cherries.

Just the smell of meat cooking over charcoal awakens the taste buds and even the humbler sausages and beefburgers are so much more delicious when cooked in this way. As well as the usual chops and chicken drumsticks, spicy foods such as spare ribs and kebabs are ideal for a barbecue. Look out for the Greek 'pitta' bread, which when halved forms pockets to put the barbecued kebabs in, making them much easier to eat. After this spicy food, a refreshing fruit salad makes a perfect end to the meal.

Lunch or Supper

(JUNE)

CHICKEN AND AVOCADO SALAD

HOT NEW POTATOES

BLACKCURRANT ICE CREAM

Chicken and Avocado Salad

SERVES 4

4 chicken breasts
2 garlic cloves
6 rashers streaky bacon, rinded
    and diced
225 g (8 oz) button
    mushrooms, washed
rind and juice of 1 lemon
3-4 tablespoons olive oil
salt
freshly ground black pepper
1 avocado
2 tablespoons chopped fresh
    parsley

PREPARATION TIME: *20 minutes*

COOKING TIME: *40 minutes*

The stock which results from
simmering the chicken
breasts will be well-flavoured
after 40 minutes and should
be reserved for use in soups.

1. Put the chicken breasts
into a saucepan of lightly
salted water with the lemon
rind and 1 garlic clove. Bring
to the boil and simmer for 40
minutes. Leave to cool in the
liquid.
2. Fry the bacon until crisp.
Leave to cool.
3. When the chicken is cold,
strain, (reserving the cooking
liquor if desired for later use
in soups) discarding the
lemon rind and garlic.
Remove the skin and bones
and cut the flesh into large
chunks. Arrange on a shallow
serving dish, interspersed
with the mushrooms.
4. Crush the other clove of
garlic. Reserve 1 tablespoon
of lemon juice. Mix the rest
with the garlic, olive oil and
salt and pepper and pour
over the chicken and
mushrooms.
5. Peel and slice the
avocado, brush with the
reserved lemon juice, and
place slices in a circle around
the edge of the chicken and
mushrooms.
6. Sprinkle the bacon over
the centre of the dish. Cover
the whole dish with chopped
parsley. Serve with hot new
potatoes.

Blackcurrant Ice Cream

SERVES 6

225 g (8 oz) blackcurrants
100 g (4 oz) caster sugar
3 tablespoons Cassis
2 tablespoons water
4 eggs, separated
300 ml (½ pint) double or
    whipping cream, whipped

PREPARATION TIME: *15 minutes,*
    plus freezing

COOKING TIME: *5-10 minutes*

Cassis is a French
blackcurrant liqueur which
gives this ice cream an
exquisite flavour. As well as
flavouring blackcurrant
dishes, a little Cassis mixed
with a glass of white wine
makes a delicious summer
drink called Kir.

1. Put the blackcurrants into
a pan with the sugar, Cassis
and water. Gently bring to the
boil, stir well until the sugar
has dissolved, then cook until
the fruit is soft. Press through
a sieve to make a thick purée.
Cool.
2. Whisk the egg yolks and
blackcurrant purée with the
cream.
3. Whisk the egg whites until
stiff, then lightly fold into the
mixture. Pour into a rigid
container, cover and freeze
for at least 2-3 hours.

VARIATION:

This recipe uses
blackcurrants but other fruit
can be puréed and used in
the same way.
    Try serving a fruit ice
cream with a complementary
fruit purée – peach ice cream
with a raspberry purée, for
example.

Evening Meal
JUNE

GOUJONS OF TROUT
WITH HAZELNUTS

CHEESE AND WATERCRESS SOUFFLÉ

TOMATOES PROVENÇALE

CHERRY GÂTEAU CARDINALE

Goujons of Trout with Hazelnuts

SERVES 4

2 trout, skinned and filleted
50 g (2 oz) hazelnuts, skinned
* and chopped*
100 g (4 oz) fresh white
* breadcrumbs*
25 g (1 oz) seasoned flour
2 eggs, beaten
oil, for deep-frying
1 grapefruit, skinned and
* segmented*

PREPARATION TIME: *15 minutes,*
* plus chilling*

COOKING TIME: *10 minutes*

1. Cut the trout into strips diagonally.
2. Mix together the chopped hazelnuts and breadcrumbs in a bowl.
3. Coat the fish with the seasoned flour, dip in the egg, then roll in the breadcrumb mixture. Chill for about 30 minutes.
4. Deep-fry in the hot oil in 2 batches for about 5 minutes each batch.
5. Drain well on kitchen paper, keeping the first batch hot while the other batch is cooking. Divide between 4 plates and serve with the grapefruit segments.

Cheese and Watercress Soufflé

SERVES 4

25 g (1 oz) butter
25 g (1 oz) plain flour
300 ml (½ pint) milk
50 g (2 oz) Cheddar cheese,
  grated
25 g (1 oz) Parmesan cheese,
  grated
1 bunch watercress, stalks
  removed
3 eggs, separated
salt
freshly ground black pepper
butter, for greasing

PREPARATION TIME: *15 minutes*

COOKING TIME: *40-50 minutes*

OVEN: *180°C, 350°F, Gas Mark 4*

1. Melt the butter in a pan, stir in the flour and cook for 2-3 minutes.
2. Add the milk gradually, bring to the boil, stirring all the time, and cook for 2-3 minutes. Remove from the heat and add the Cheddar cheese and most of the Parmesan.
3. Reserve a few sprigs of watercress for garnish, then chop the rest, add to the sauce with the egg yolks, salt and pepper.
4. Whisk the egg whites until stiff, then fold lightly into the sauce.
5. Butter well an 18 cm (7 inch) soufflé dish and sprinkle with the reserved Parmesan cheese.
6. Pour the mixture into the soufflé dish. Cook in a preheated oven for 40-50 minutes. Tomatoes provençale (tomatoes cut in half and sprinkled with breadcrumbs, crushed garlic and chopped parsley) can be cooked in the oven at the same temperature for the last 10 minutes of the soufflé cooking time.
7. Garnish with the reserved watercress sprigs and serve immediately with tomatoes provençale.

NOTE:
The base of the soufflé can be made in advance leaving just the egg whites to be folded in immediately before cooking.

When watercress is unavailable, 100 g (4 oz) chopped cooked spinach can be used instead.

Cherry Gâteau Cardinale

SERVES 4-6

*100 g (4 oz) soft margarine, at
  room temperature*
100 g (4 oz) self-raising flour
100 g (4 oz) caster sugar
2 eggs, beaten
1 teaspoon baking powder
½ teaspoon almond essence
*300 ml (½ pint) double or
  whipping cream, whipped*
*100 g (4 oz) ripe red cherries,
  stoned and halved*
*50 g (2 oz) flaked almonds,
  toasted*
100 g (4 oz) redcurrant jelly

PREPARATION TIME: *40 minutes*

COOKING TIME: *30-35 minutes*

OVEN: *180°C, 350°F, Gas Mark 4*

1. Grease and line two 18 cm (7 inch) sandwich tins.
2. Put the margarine, flour, sugar, eggs, baking powder and almond essence in a mixing bowl and whisk for 2-3 minutes until the mixture is light and fluffy.
3. Divide the mixture between the 2 tins. Bake in a preheated oven for 30-35 minutes. Turn the cakes out on to a wire tray to cool.
4. Mix half the cream with the cherries and use to sandwich the cakes together.
5. Spread a little of the remaining cream around the side of the gâteau and either press the almonds on to the cream, using a palette knife or place the almonds on a chopping board and roll the cake in them to coat.
6. Melt the redcurrant jelly in a pan over a gentle heat. Whisk until smooth. Cool until almost set, then pour over the top to within 1 cm (½ inch) of the edge.
7. Put the remaining cream into a piping bag with a star nozzle and pipe around the edge of the redcurrant jelly.

VARIATION:
Any fresh, frozen or canned soft fruit can be used. For raspberries, strawberries and redcurrants, the redcurrant jelly can be used for the topping, but for apricots or peaches, use an equal amount of sieved apricot jam.

Dinner Party
(JUNE)

AVOCADO, MANGO AND
GRAPEFRUIT COCKTAIL

SALMON STEAKS WITH FENNEL

POTATO NESTS WITH TOMATO

MANGE-TOUT PEAS

ENDIVE AND BACON SALAD

APRICOT AND ALMOND SAVARIN

Avocado, Mango and Grapefruit Cocktail with Blue Cheese Dressing

SERVES 4

2 tablespoons mayonnaise
1 tablespoon oil
2 teaspoons white wine vinegar
salt
freshly ground black pepper
50 g (2 oz) blue cheese
1 avocado, peeled and diced
1 mango, peeled and diced
2 grapefruit, peeled and
   segmented

PREPARATION TIME: *10 minutes*

1. Mix together the mayonnaise, oil, vinegar, salt and pepper. Grate or crumble in the blue cheese and mix well.
2. Put the avocado, mango and grapefruit into a bowl. Pour in the dressing, toss lightly then divide between 4 dishes. Serve chilled.

Endive and Bacon Salad

SERVES 4

1 curly endive, washed
100 g (4 oz) streaky bacon,
   rinded and diced
2-3 tablespoons oil
1 thick slice bread, crusts
   removed and cut into cubes
1 tablespoon wine vinegar

PREPARATION TIME: *10 minutes*

COOKING TIME: *10 minutes*

This simple salad makes a refreshing course between a meat dish and dessert. Add the dressing just before serving.

1. Put the endive into a wooden salad bowl.
2. Fry the bacon, remove and keep warm. Add the oil to the pan and fry the bread until brown on all sides.
3. Dress the endive with the wine vinegar then add the hot bacon, fried bread and any remaining oil to the salad. Toss well and serve while still warm.

VARIATION:
Add a tablespoon of walnut or hazelnut oil for extra flavour.

Salmon Steaks with Fennel

SERVES 4

2 heads Florence fennel
2 salmon steaks, about 750 g
    (1½ lb) total, skinned,
    boned and each piece cut in
    half horizontally to make 4
salt
freshly ground white pepper
150 ml (¼ pint) fish stock
150 ml (¼ pint) dry white
    wine
1 tablespoon softened butter
1 tablespoon plain flour
2 tablespoons double cream

PREPARATION TIME: *15 minutes*

COOKING TIME: *45 minutes*

OVEN: *180°C, 350°F, Gas Mark 4*

If possible get the fishmonger to prepare the salmon for this dish. If it is not possible to get the salmon steaks it can be made with the conventional salmon cutlets.

1. Trim the fennel, cut into 4 slices downwards, reserving the leaves. Cook in lightly salted water for about 15 minutes.
2. Drain the fennel well, then place in a shallow ovenproof dish. Lay the salmon on top. Sprinkle with salt and pepper. Pour the fish stock and wine over the top of the salmon. Cover the dish with foil. Cook in a preheated oven for 20 minutes.
3. Remove the foil, lifting it from the side furthest away from you, to prevent the steam rising in your face. Transfer each salmon steak with the fennel underneath on to a warmed serving dish. Keep warm, whilst making the sauce.
4. Put the fish stock and wine into a small saucepan. Mix the butter and flour together and add, a little at a time, to the saucepan. Bring to the boil, whisking well. Cook for 2-3 minutes, then add the double cream.
5. Pour over the salmon and garnish with the fennel leaves.
6. Serve with Potato nests with tomato (see below) and mange-tout peas.

Potato Nests with Tomato

SERVES 4

450 g (1 lb) potatoes, peeled
50 g (2 oz) butter
1 egg, beaten
salt
freshly ground black pepper
2 small tomatoes, sliced into 4

PREPARATION TIME: *20 minutes,*
    plus cooling

COOKING TIME: *55 minutes*

OVEN: *180°C, 350°F, Gas Mark 4*

1. Boil the potatoes in salted water until soft. Strain, mash well, then sieve to remove lumps. Beat in most of the butter with the egg, salt and pepper. Leave the mixture until cold.
2. Grease a baking sheet with the remaining butter. Put the potatoes into a piping bag fitted with a star nozzle and pipe 8 nest shapes on to the baking sheet. Put a slice of tomato in the centre of each potato nest.
3. Cook in a preheated oven for 35 minutes.

Apricot and Almond Savarin

SERVES 4

15 g (½ oz) fresh yeast
15 g (½ oz) caster sugar
3 tablespoons warm milk
100 g (4 oz) plain flour, plus 2 teaspoons, for dusting
¼ teaspoon salt
2 eggs, beaten
50 g (2 oz) softened butter
lard, for greasing

FILLING AND GLAZE:

100 g (4 oz) granulated sugar
300 ml (½ pint) water
450 g (1 lb) apricots, halved and stoned
2 tablespoons rum
25 g (1 oz) whole blanched almonds
3 tablespoons apricot jam
2 tablespoons water
150 ml (¼ pint) double or whipping cream, whipped, to serve

PREPARATION TIME: *30 minutes, plus proving*

COOKING TIME: *1 hour*

OVEN: *200°C, 400°F, Gas Mark 6*

1. Put the yeast and sugar into a small bowl, add the milk and stir until the yeast has dissolved.
2. Sieve 25 g (1 oz) of the flour on to the yeast mixture and blend to a smooth paste. Put the bowl over a pan of boiling water off the heat for 15-20 minutes, until the mixture is spongy.
3. Sieve the remaining flour and salt into a large bowl, add the yeast mixture and eggs and gradually work in the flour. Add the butter, a little at a time, and beat well for 3-4 minutes until the mixture forms long strands.
4. Grease a 900 ml (1½ pint) ring mould with the lard and dust with flour. Put the mixture into the tin, place in a polythene bag and leave in a warm place for about 30 minutes until the mixture reaches the top of the mould.
5. Remove the bag. Place the mould in a preheated oven for 20 minutes. Remove from the oven, cool for a few minutes, then turn out on to a wire tray with a large plate underneath. Prick well.
6. For the filling, put the sugar and water in a pan, stir until the sugar has dissolved, then bring to the boil. Poach the apricots in the syrup for about 10 minutes until soft, then cool in the syrup.
7. Strain the apricots, add the rum to the syrup and pour over the savarin, pouring over again any syrup that goes on to the plate.
8. Transfer the savarin to a serving plate. Reserve 6 apricots for decoration and fill the centre of the savarin with the rest.
9. Put a whole almond in the centre of each reserved apricot. Place the rest in the centre of the apricots on top of the savarin.
10. Put the jam in a small saucepan, add the water and bring to the boil. Glaze the savarin with the jam. Glaze the reserved apricots with jam.
11. Put half the cream in a piping bag with a large star nozzle. Pipe 6 whirls of cream around the top of the savarin, put the reserved apricots on top of the whirls of cream. Serve with the remaining cream.

VARIATION:
Although it will not be an authentic savarin, if the thought of making this yeast cake base seems daunting, a similar dessert can be made by making a basic sponge mixture in a ring mould for the base. Alternatively, the yeast mixture can be made in individual ring moulds to make rum babas. These would take only 10-15 minutes to cook.

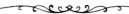

Lunch or Supper

(JULY)

TUNA STUFFED PEPPERS

STONE CREAM WITH PEACHES
AND RATAFIAS

Tuna-Stuffed Peppers

SERVES 4

4 medium green peppers, tops
   removed, cored and seeded
1 x 200 g (7 oz) can tuna fish in
   oil
1 small onion, chopped
12 stuffed olives, sliced
2 tomatoes, skinned, seeded
   and chopped
100 g (4 oz) cooked rice
salt
freshly ground black pepper
1 x 326 g (11½ oz) can
   sweetcorn kernels

PREPARATION TIME: *25 minutes*

COOKING TIME: *50-55 minutes*

OVEN: *180°C, 350°F, Gas Mark 4*

Stuffed peppers are always
attractive. The sweetcorn
adds both colour and texture.

1. Put the peppers and their
tops into a pan, cover with
water, bring to the boil,
simmer for 5 minutes, then
drain well.
2. Drain the tuna fish,
reserving the oil. Fry the
onion until soft in 1
tablespoon of the tuna oil.
3. Mix together the olives,
tomatoes, tuna, rice, onion,
salt and pepper. Divide the
mixture between the
peppers. Replace the lids.
4. Put the peppers into an
overproof dish and drizzle
the remaining tuna oil over
the top. Cover with a lid or
foil. Cook in a preheated
oven for 40-45 minutes.
5. Heat the sweetcorn, put
into a shallow dish, and
arrange the peppers on top.

Stone Cream with Peaches

SERVES 4

*2 ripe peaches, skinned and
   sliced*
50 g (2 oz) ratafia biscuits
3 teaspoons powdered gelatine
3 tablespoons water
300 ml (½ pint) cold milk
15 g (½ oz) caster sugar
*150 ml (¼ pint) double or
   whipping cream, whipped*
1 egg white
4 Ratafia biscuits, to decorate

PREPARATION TIME: *15 minutes,
   plus setting*

COOKING TIME: *5 minutes*

Stone cream is an old English
traditional dessert, usually
with jam underneath. This
version uses fresh peaches as
a delicious alternative.

1. Divide the peaches and
ratafias between 4 dessert
dishes.
2. Dissolve the gelatine in
the water. Heat the milk and
sugar in a small pan until the
sugar has dissolved. Stir in
the gelatine. Chill until cold
and starting to set, about 30
minutes.
3. Fold the cream into the
milk. Whisk the egg white
until stiff and fold into the
cream mixture. Pour over the
peaches and ratafias.
Decorate with ratafias. Leave
until set.

VARIATION:
The peaches can be
substituted with any fresh soft
fruit and, in winter, canned or
frozen fruit can be used.

Ratafias

MAKES ABOUT 24

1 egg white
75 g (3 oz) ground almonds
75 oz (3 oz) caster sugar
½ teaspoon almond essence

PREPARATION TIME: *10 minutes*

COOKING TIME: *15-20 minutes*

OVEN: *180°C, 350°F, Gas Mark 4*

1. Line 1-2 baking sheets
with non-stick silicone or
lightly greased greaseproof
paper.
2. Whisk the egg white until
stiff, then add the ground
almonds, sugar and almond
essence.
3. Spoon the mixture into a
piping bag fitted with a 5 mm
(¼ inch) plain nozzle, then
pipe small blobs on to the
prepared baking sheets.
4. Cook in a preheated oven
for 15-20 minutes, until
brown and crisp. Remove to a
wire tray to cool. Use to
decorate the Stone cream
(see left).

Evening Meal
JULY

SALMAGUNDI

MACKEREL WITH GOOSEBERRIES
NEW POTATOES

LEMON SOUFFLÉ PANCAKES
WITH RASPBERRY SAUCE

Salmagundi

SERVES 4

50 g (2 oz) cooked ham, cut
   into strips
1 cooked chicken breast,
   skinned, boned and cut into
   strips
2 sticks celery, cut into strips
1 small red dessert apple, cored,
   sliced and cut into strips
50 g (2 oz) walnuts, chopped
3 tablespoons mayonnaise
1 tablespoon oil
juice of ½ lemon
salt
freshly ground black pepper

TO GARNISH:
lettuce
4 small tomatoes, cut into
   quarters
4 sprigs parsley

PREPARATION TIME: *10 minutes*

1. Mix together the ham,
chicken, celery, apple and
walnuts.
2. Whisk together the
mayonnaise, oil, lemon juice,
salt and pepper. Lightly fold
into the ham and chicken
mixture.
3. Line 4 small plates with
lettuce leaves. Divide the
mixture between the plates.
Garnish with tomatoes and
parsley.

Mackerel with Gooseberries

SERVES 4

2 large mackerel, filleted
100 g (4 oz) gooseberries,
   topped and tailed
150 ml (¼ pint) dry cider
150 ml (¼ pint) milk
salt
freshly ground black pepper
15 g (½ oz) butter
15 g (½ oz) plain flour

PREPARATION TIME: *10 minutes*

COOKING TIME: *25 minutes*

OVEN: *180°C, 350°F, Gas Mark 4*

1. Put the mackerel fillets
into a shallow ovenproof
dish. Add the gooseberries.
Pour the cider and milk over
and sprinkle with salt and
pepper. Cover the dish with
foil. Cook in a preheated
oven for 20 minutes.
2. When the fish is cooked,
carefully strain off the liquid.
Keep the fish and
gooseberries warm.
3. Melt the butter in a small
pan, stir in the flour and cook
for 2-3 minutes. Pour in the
cider and milk, bring to the
boil, stirring well, then cook
for 2-3 minutes. Pour the
sauce over the fish.
4. Serve with new potatoes.

Lemon Soufflé Pancakes with Raspberry Sauce

SERVES 4

PANCAKES:
50 g (2 oz) plain flour, sifted
1 egg, beaten
200 ml (⅓ pint) milk
lard, for greasing

LEMON SOUFFLÉ FILLING:
25 g (1 oz) butter
25 g (1 oz) plain flour
300 ml (½ pint) milk
25 g (1 oz) caster sugar
grated rind and juice of
*   1 lemon*
2 eggs, separated
1 egg white
25 g (1 oz) icing sugar

SAUCE:
225 g (8 oz) raspberries
50 g (2 oz) icing sugar
juice of 1 lemon

PREPARATION TIME: *20 minutes*

COOKING TIME: *40 minutes*

OVEN: *200°C, 400°F, Gas Mark 6*

1. Put the flour into a mixing bowl, beat in the egg and milk to make a thin batter. Grease a 15 cm (6 inch) frying pan and make 8 small pancakes, then set aside.
2. To make the filling, melt the butter in a pan, stir in the flour and cook for 2-3 minutes. Stir in the milk, sugar, lemon rind and juice. Bring to the boil, stirring well, then cook for 2-3 minutes. Cool slightly, then beat in the egg yolks.
3. Whisk the egg whites until stiff, then lightly fold into the mixture.
4. Put 1 tablespoonful of the lemon mixture into each pancake, then fold it over. Sift a little icing sugar over each.
5. Place in a preheated oven for 10-15 minutes. Serve hot.
6. To make the sauce, sieve the raspberries into a bowl, then add the icing sugar and lemon juice and mix well.

NOTE:
If making the pancakes well in advance, it is a good idea to layer them with greaseproof paper to stop them sticking together.

The lemon soufflé filling can be made in advance up to the end of stage 3 with the egg whites folded in just before assembling.

For a variation substitute the lemon filling with 300 ml (½ pint) thick pear purée made by putting the drained contents of a 410 g (14½ oz) can pears into a blender or food processor then liquidizing them. Make the purée up to 300 ml (½ pint) with some of the syrup from the can if necessary. Add the egg yolks and whites and proceed as for the basic recipe. These pear pancakes are delicious if served with chocolate sauce.

Summer Barbecue

JULY

SPICED LAMB KEBABS
PARMESAN CHICKEN DRUMSTICKS
BARBECUED SPARE RIBS
TABBOULEH
MIXED SALAD
PITTA BREAD

WHITE WINE CUP

SUMMER FRUIT SALAD

As all the cooking for the barbecue is done at the last minute, this menu is designed so that as much preparation as possible is completed in advance, taking advantage of the fact that most of the items positively benefit from being left to marinate. As long as they are left, covered, in a refrigerator or a very cool place, both the Spiced Lamb Kebabs and Barbecued Spare Ribs can be prepared the day before. Also making the Tabbouleh the day before really brings out the flavour of the mint and parsley. The fruit salad can be made earlier in the day of the barbecue, leaving out the strawberries to be added at the last minute.

CLOCKWISE FROM THE LEFT:
Parmesan chicken drumsticks; Mixed salad;
Tabbouleh; Barbecued spare ribs, Spiced lamb
kebabs (recipes page 68)

Spiced Lamb Kebabs

SERVES 8

1 medium onion, peeled and
  chopped
1 garlic clove, peeled
1 x 150 ml (5 fl oz) carton
  plain unsweetened yogurt
25 g (1 oz) cream of coconut
juice of ½ lemon
1 tablespoon oil
1 teaspoon ground coriander
2 teaspoons ground cumin
1 teaspoon garam masala
½ teaspoon chilli powder
2 teaspoons turmeric
½ teaspoon mixed spice
salt
freshly ground black pepper
1 kg (2 lb) boned lamb, cut into
  cubes

PREPARATION TIME: *20 minutes*
COOKING TIME: *15-20 minutes*

1. Put the onion, garlic, yogurt, cream of coconut, lemon juice and oil into a blender or food processor. Blend until smooth. Pour into a large bowl.
2. Add the coriander, cumin, garam masala, chilli, turmeric, mixed spice, salt and pepper.
3. Add the cubes of lamb to the spice mixture. Stir well to coat, then leave in a cool place for 2-3 hours.
4. Thread the lamb cubes on to skewers and cook over charcoal for 15-20 minutes, turning frequently.
(Pictured on page 67.)

NOTE:
A boned shoulder of lamb would be ideal for this dish.

Parmesan Chicken Drumsticks

SERVES 8

50 g (2 oz) fresh white
  breadcrumbs
50 g (2 oz) Parmesan cheese,
  grated
8 large chicken drumsticks,
  skinned
2 tablespoons seasoned flour
2 eggs, beaten

PREPARATION TIME: *15 minutes*
COOKING TIME: *30-40 minutes*

1. Skin the chicken. Mix together the breadcrumbs and Parmesan cheese.
2. Coat the drumsticks with the seasoned flour, dip in the egg, then roll in the breadcrumbs. Chill for 30 minutes.
3. Cook over charcoal for 30-40 minutes, turning frequently.
(Pictured on page 66.)

VARIATION:
As a crunchy alternative the Parmesan cheese can be substituted with 50 g (2 oz) of finely chopped peanuts.

Barbecued Spare Ribs

SERVES 8

1.75 kg (4 lb) pork spare ribs
2 tablespoons vinegar

SAUCE:
4 tablespoons tomato ketchup
4 tablespoons clear honey
4 tablespoons soy sauce
1 tablespoon wine vinegar
1 teaspoon English mustard
  powder
150 ml (¼ pint) water
1 tablespoon Worcestershire
  sauce
1 teaspoon paprika
salt
freshly ground black pepper
lemon slices, to garnish

PREPARATION TIME: *25 minutes*
COOKING TIME: *30 minutes*

1. Put the spare ribs and vinegar into a large pan of salted water, bring to the boil and simmer for 15 minutes.
2. Meanwhile put all the sauce ingredients into a pan, stir well, bring to the boil and simmer for 5 minutes.
3. Strain the spare ribs, put into a large bowl and pour the sauce over. Leave until cool, turning frequently.
4. Strain off the sauce. Cook the spare ribs over charcoal for 10-15 minutes. Garnish with lemon slices. Reheat the sauce and serve separately.
(Pictured on page 67.)

VARIATION:
Instead of spare ribs, this dish can be made with thin slices of lean belly pork.

Tabbouleh

SERVES 8

350 g (12 oz) bulghar or
  cracked wheat
2 bunches spring onions, finely
  chopped
1 large bunch parsley, chopped
1 large bunch mint, chopped
juice of 2 lemons
150 ml (¼ pint) olive oil
salt
freshly ground black pepper

PREPARATION TIME: *10 minutes,*
  plus soaking

1. Put the bulghar into a large bowl and cover with plenty of cold water. Soak for 1 hour. Strain well, pressing out as much water as possible.
2. Put the bulghar back into the bowl, and add the spring onions, parsley, mint, lemon juice, olive oil, salt and pepper. Mix well.
(Pictured on page 67.)

NOTE:
Bulghar is available at most health food shops.

Mixed Salad

SERVES 8

1 large crispy lettuce, washed
225 g (8 oz) tomatoes,
  quartered
2 red peppers, cored and seeded
2-3 avocados, peeled and sliced
150 ml (¼ pint) French
  dressing

PREPARATION TIME: *10 minutes*

1. Break up the lettuce into a large bowl and add the tomatoes. Slice the peppers and add to the salad together with the avocados.
2. Pour in the French dressing and toss lightly. Serve with pitta bread.
(Pictured on page 67.)

White Wine cup

SERVES 8

4 tablespoons brandy
1 orange, sliced
1 lemon, sliced
3 bottles dry white wine
1 x 1 litre (1¾ pint) bottle
 lemonade

PREPARATION TIME: *10 minutes,*
 plus soaking

1. Pour the brandy over the orange and lemon slices in a large punch bowl. Leave for 30 minutes.
2. Pour in the wine and lemonade. Chill well.

Summer Fruit Salad

SERVES 8

175 g (6 oz) caster sugar
300 ml (½ pint) water
450 g (1 lb) blackcurrants
225 g (8 oz) raspberries
450 g (1 lb) cherries, stoned
3 tablespoons Cassis
225 g (8 oz) strawberries

PREPARATION TIME: *15 minutes*

COOKING TIME: *5 minutes*

1. Dissolve the sugar in the water, add the blackcurrants. Simmer gently for about 5 minutes until the fruit is soft.
2. Pour into a large bowl, add the raspberries, cherries and Cassis. Chill well. Just before serving lightly stir in the strawberries.

TOP TO BOTTOM: *White wine cup;*
Summer fruit salad

Dinner Party

JULY

MONKFISH AURORE

LOIN OF LAMB STUFFED WITH
CUCUMBER AND MINT

SAUCE PALOISE

NEW POTATOES

BROAD BEANS

STRAWBERRY CHEESECAKE GÂTEAU

Monkfish Aurore

SERVES 4

450 g (1 lb) monkfish
150 ml (¼ pint) mayonnaise
3 tablespoons double or
  whipping cream, whipped
1 tablespoon lemon juice
1 teaspoon tomato purée
1 tablespoon chopped capers
1 tablespoon chopped gherkins
salt
freshly ground black pepper

TO GARNISH:
4 gherkin fans
4 lemon slices

PREPARATION TIME: *20 minutes*
COOKING TIME: *10 minutes*

1. Cut the monkfish into 2.5 cm (1 inch) cubes, put into a pan of lightly salted water, bring to the boil and simmer for 10 minutes. Remove from the heat and leave to cool in the liquid.
2. In a bowl mix together the mayonnaise, cream, lemon juice, tomato purée, capers, gherkins, salt and pepper.
3. Strain the cooled fish and add to the mayonnaise mixture. Divide between 4 plates and garnish with gherkins and lemon slices.

NOTE:
Monkfish can be fried in batter as an inexpensive scampi dish.

Loin of Lamb stuffed with Cucumber and Mint

SERVES 4

2 shallots, chopped
15 g (½ oz) butter
100 g (4 oz) cucumber, peeled and grated
1 tablespoon chopped fresh mint
50 g (2 oz) fresh white breadcrumbs
1 egg yolk
salt
freshly ground black pepper
1 boned loin of lamb, 1 kg (2 lb) boned weight

PREPARATION TIME: *20 minutes*

COOKING TIME: *1½ hours*

OVEN: *180°C, 350°F, Gas Mark 4*

1. Fry the shallot in the butter until soft, add the cucumber, mint, breadcrumbs, egg yolk, salt and pepper. Mix well, then leave to cool.
2. Lay the lamb out and score the fat in a diamond pattern. Turn over and spread the stuffing over the meat. Roll up and tie with string.
3. Cook in a preheated oven for about 1½ hours. Remove the string before serving with the Sauce paloise (see right) handed separately.
4. New potatoes and broad beans go well with this dish.

Sauce Paloise

SERVES 4

4 tablespoons wine vinegar
2 tablespoons water
1 teaspoon dried mint
6 black peppercorns
1 shallot, chopped
2 egg yolks
75 g (3 oz) unsalted butter
1 tablespoon chopped fresh mint
salt

PREPARATION TIME: *10 minutes*

COOKING TIME: *10 minutes*

This is a variation of the classic Béarnaise sauce with mint used instead of tarragon, thus echoing the flavour of the lamb stuffing.

1. Put the vinegar, water, dried mint, peppercorns and shallot into a pan. Boil until reduced to 2 tablespoons. Strain well.
2. Put the egg yolks in the top of a double saucepan or in a bowl over a pan of simmering water and whisk in the vinegar mixture until the mixture is light and fluffy. Take care that the water underneath does not boil.
3. Add the butter, a little at a time, whisking well. Stir in the fresh mint. Add salt to taste. Serve the sauce warm with the loin of lamb.

Strawberry Cheesecake Gâteau

SERVES 4-6

SPONGE BASE:
50 g (2 oz) soft margarine at room temperature
50 g (2 oz) self-raising flour, sifted
½ teaspoon baking powder
1 egg
50 g (2 oz) caster sugar
225 g (8 oz) strawberries

CHEESECAKE FILLING:
350 g (12 oz) curd cheese
75 g (3 oz) caster sugar
15 g (½ oz) powdered gelatine
3 tablespoons water
1 teaspoon vanilla essence
200 ml (⅓ pint) double or whipping cream, whipped
3 egg whites, stiffly whisked

TO DECORATE:
1 tablespoon sifted icing sugar
85 ml (3 fl oz) double or whipping cream, stiffly whipped

PREPARATION TIME: *45 minutes, plus setting*

COOKING TIME: *20 minutes*

OVEN: *180°C, 350°F, Gas Mark 4*

1. Grease and line an 18 cm (7 inch) sandwich tin. Place the margarine, flour, baking powder, egg and sugar in a mixing bowl and whisk until light and fluffy. Cook in a preheated oven for 20 minutes. Turn out on to a wire tray to cool.

2. Mix the curd cheese with the caster sugar. Dissolve the gelatine in the water over a gentle heat and add to the cheese with the vanilla essence. Fold in the whipped cream. Lightly fold the whisked egg whites into the cheese mixture.

3. Lightly oil the sides of a 16 cm (6½ inch) loose-based cake tin. Cut the sponge in half horizontally and place the bottom half in the tin.

4. Reserving 6 strawberries for decoration, slice the rest on to the sponge base. Pour in the cheesecake mixture and top with the reserved sponge. Chill until set.

5. When set, carefully remove from the tin. Dust the top with sifted icing sugar. Decorate with whirls of cream and the reserved strawberries.

VARIATIONS:
Cheesecakes make a very versatile dessert with many variations. There are many types of soft cheese now on the market and most are suitable for cheesecakes. Curd cheese, cottage cheese if sieved and skimmed milk soft cheese are all good for keeping the calories down. If full-fat soft cheese is used, half the cream in the recipe can be substituted with plain unsweetened yogurt.

The strawberries in the recipe can be substituted with any other soft fruit or to make a lemon cheesecake omit the vanilla essence and add the grated rind and juice of 2 lemons but add a further ½ teaspoon of powdered gelatine.

If a biscuit crumb base is preferred rather than the sponge base, crumble 175 g (6 oz) digestive biscuits, mix with 50 g (2 oz) caster sugar and 50 g (2 oz) melted butter. Put half the mixture into the base of the tin then sprinkle the rest over the top.

Lunch or Supper
(AUGUST)

CORN CHOWDER

GRANARY ROLLS

SOFT CHEESE, E.G. BRIE OR CHEVRE,
FRESH FIGS AND BATH OLIVERS

Corn Chowder

SERVES 4

25 g (1 oz) butter
1 medium onion, peeled and
    chopped
1 small green pepper, cored,
    seeded and sliced
100 g (4 oz) button
    mushrooms, sliced
1 tablespoon plain flour
300 ml (½ pint) light stock
300 ml (½ pint) milk
1 x 425 g (15 oz) can sweetcorn
2 medium potatoes, peeled and
    diced
salt
freshly ground black pepper
1 x 150 ml (5 fl oz) carton
    single cream

PREPARATION TIME: *10 minutes*
COOKING TIME: *35 minutes*

1. Melt the butter in a pan, add the onion, pepper and mushrooms and cook for 2-3 minutes.
2. Stir in the flour and cook for 2 minutes, then add the stock, milk, sweetcorn with the liquid from the can, potatoes, salt and pepper.
3. Bring to the boil and simmer for 30 minutes. Add the cream to the pan and reheat without boiling. Serve with granary rolls.

VARIATION:
When in season this soup can be made with fresh corn cobs. Boil them in unsalted water for 10-15 minutes, then scrape the corn from the husks with a sharp knife.

Evening Meal

AUGUST

SWEET AND SOUR CUCUMBER

VEAL AND PEPPER CASSEROLE

NOODLES

PLUM AND ALMOND CRISP

Sweet and Sour Cucumber

SERVES 4

1 cucumber, sliced
salt

DRESSING:
1 small onion, finely chopped
2 tablespoons white wine
  vinegar
1 tablespoon clear honey
5 tablespoons oil
2 tablespoons tomato purée
1 tablespoon English mustard
  powder
salt
freshly ground black pepper
coriander leaf, to garnish

PREPARATION TIME: *10 minutes,*
  plus salting

1. Put the cucumber into a colander. Sprinkle with salt, put a plate on top and leave for 30 minutes.
2. Rinse the cucumber and dry well. Arrange in a serving dish.
3. Mix together all the dressing ingredients. Pour over the cucumber. Garnish with coriander and chill well.

NOTE:
The reason for the 'salting' in this recipe is to bring out the natural moisture from the cucumber, otherwise it would make the dressing too watery.

Veal and Pepper Casserole

SERVES 4

750 g (1½ lb) stewing veal, cut
    into cubes
2-3 tablespoons seasoned flour
1 onion, peeled and sliced
2 tablespoons oil
about 3 teaspoons paprika
salt
freshly ground black pepper
300 ml (½ pint) light stock
1 large red pepper, cored,
    seeded and cut into strips
1 large green pepper, cored,
    seeded and cut into strips
100 g (4 oz) button
    mushrooms, sliced
1 x 150 ml (5 fl oz) carton
    soured cream

PREPARATION TIME: *15 minutes*

COOKING TIME: *1¾ hours*

OVEN: *160°C, 325°F, Gas Mark 3*

1. Coat the veal in the seasoned flour. In a flameproof casserole fry the onion in the oil until soft, then add the veal to the pan and brown the cubes.
2. Add 2 teaspoons of the paprika to the pan, cook for 2-3 minutes, then add salt and pepper to taste and the stock. Bring to the boil, cover the pan, place in a preheated oven and cook for 1 hour.
3. Remove the casserole from the oven, add the peppers, mushrooms and most of the soured cream. Return to the oven and cook for a further 30 minutes.
4. Put the reserved soured cream on top, sprinkle with the remaining paprika and serve with hot buttered noodles.

Plum and Almond Crisp

SERVES 4

50 g (2 oz) butter
100 g (4 oz) soft white
    breadcrumbs
50 g (2 oz) soft brown sugar
50 g (2 oz) flaked almonds
½ teaspoon ground cinnamon
450 g (1 lb) plums, stoned and
    lightly poached
whipping or double cream,
    whipped, to serve

PREPARATION TIME: *20 minutes,
    plus cooling*

COOKING TIME: *35-40 minutes*

OVEN: *180°C, 350°F, Gas Mark 4*

1. Melt the butter in a pan. Stir in the breadcrumbs, sugar, almonds and cinnamon.
2. Put the plums in a pie dish, then sprinkle the breadcrumb mixture over the top. Bake in a preheated oven for 30-35 minutes. Serve cold with the cream.

VARIATION:

This is a very versatile recipe with many variations. The plums can be substituted with lightly poached apples or rhubarb and instead of flaked almonds, try using chopped walnuts or Brazil nuts.

Prue Leith's Dinner Party

AUGUST

PUMPKIN AND LEMON SOUP

CHICKEN IN CABBAGE LEAVES
SHREDDED COURGETTES
POMMES DAUPHINOISES

SALAD OF KIWI, MANGO
AND DATES

This menu consists of a satin-smooth and tangy soup, surprisingly made with pumpkin; a simple, not expensive, main course which is full of flavour but plain; compensatingly rich potatoes; and a fresh, albeit expensive, fruit salad.

There are 35 seconds of last-minute cooking for the courgettes, but otherwise it is very simple.

Salad of kiwi, mango and dates
(recipe page 79)

Pumpkin and Lemon Soup

SERVES 6

1 large onion, peeled and sliced
50 g (2 oz) butter
450 g (1 lb) pumpkin, peeled,
    seeded and cut into chunks
225 g (½ lb) potatoes, peeled
    and sliced
1 small garlic clove, peeled and
    crushed
sprig of thyme
1.2 litres (2 pints) good
    chicken stock
salt
freshly ground black pepper
juice of 1 lemon
1 x 150 ml (5 fl oz) carton
    double cream

PREPARATION TIME: *30 minutes*

COOKING TIME: *50 minutes*

Pumpkin makes a deliciously unusual soup, which is easily and simply prepared.

1. In a large heavy saucepan slowly cook the onion in the butter until soft and transparent.
2. Add the pumpkin, potatoes, garlic and thyme. Cover the pan and cook slowly for 20 minutes or until the vegetables are soft.
3. Add the stock with salt and pepper. Bring to the boil, and simmer for 10 minutes. Remove the thyme sprig.
4. Liquidize the soup. Flavour it with lemon juice. Stir in the cream. Reheat without boiling.

Chicken in Cabbage Leaves

SERVES 6

6 cabbage leaves
6 short rashers rindless bacon
6 chicken breasts, skinned and
    boned
12 juniper berries, crushed
salt
freshly ground black pepper
melted butter

PREPARATION TIME: *30 minutes*

COOKING TIME: *45 minutes*

OVEN: *220°C, 425°F, Gas Mark 7*

If cooking the chicken at the same time as the potatoes, it can be baked at 160°C, 325°F, Gas Mark 3 for 50-60 minutes, depending on the size of the breasts.

1. Boil the cabbage leaves briefly until bright green and slightly softened. Lift out of the saucepan and drain. Lay them flat on a board and cut out the central tough stalk.
2. Lay a piece of bacon on each cabbage leaf, then add a chicken breast and sprinkle with crushed juniper berries, salt and pepper.
3. Wrap the cabbage leaves round the chicken to make neat parcels, lay them in a buttered ovenproof dish, cover with greased foil and bake in a preheated oven for 45 minutes.
4. Serve with Shredded courgettes and Pommes dauphinoises (see opposite).

Shredded Courgettes

SERVES 6

1 kg (2 lb) young courgettes
75 g (3 oz) butter
salt
freshly ground black pepper

PREPARATION TIME: *5-15 minutes*

COOKING TIME: *less than 1 minute*

1. Grate the courgettes, skin and all, on a coarse cheese grater or put through the wide julienne cutter of a processor.
2. Just before serving the chicken, melt the butter in a large frying pan (or 2 pans) and turn and toss the courgettes over moderate heat for 35 seconds only – just enough to get them hot.
3. Add salt and pepper and serve at once, before much juice runs, making them too wet.

VARIATION:
If last-minute cooking is impossible, salt the courgettes after grating them and leave to allow the juices to run. After 2 hours, squeeze them well. Then toss in the butter as above, seasoning with pepper only. Because they have already lost their excess juice, they will stay firm for 30 minutes or so in a cool oven.

Pommes Dauphinoises

SERVES 6

1 kg (2 lb) potatoes, peeled and thinly sliced
25 g (1 oz) butter
1 garlic clove, peeled and crushed
salt
freshly ground black pepper
400 ml (2/3 pint) single cream

PREPARATION TIME: *20 minutes*
COOKING TIME: *2 hours*
OVEN: *160°C, 325°F, Gas Mark 3*

1. Rinse the sliced potatoes to wash off surface starch. Dry them well.
2. Melt the butter and add the crushed garlic to it. Tip into a bowl and mix with the potato slices and salt and pepper so that they are evenly coated. Press flat in a pie dish, and pour in the cream, or enough of it just to cover the potatoes.
3. Bake in a preheated oven for 2 hours or until the potatoes are tender and the top just brown. Cooking them too fast will curdle the cream.

VARIATION:
For a more economical version of this dish, simmer the potato slices in garlic-flavoured milk until nearly cooked. Pack them into a buttered pie dish and pour over a mixture of the starchy cooking milk and single cream. Bake until tender.

Salad of Kiwi, Mango and Dates

SERVES 6

6 kiwi fruit
3 mangoes
1 box fresh dates, stoned

PREPARATION TIME: *20 minutes*

1. Peel the kiwi fruit and slice across fairly thickly.
2. Peel the mangoes as thinly as possible. Slice them in large thin slices, rather than in 'canned peach' slices.
3. Either mix with the dates in a large glass bowl or arrange a selection of the 3 on 6 dessert plates, putting the dates shiny-side up. (Pictured on page 77.)

LEFT TO RIGHT: *Pumpkin and lemon soup; Chicken in cabbage leaves; Shredded courgettes; Pommes dauphinoises*

Picnic
AUGUST

CHILLED CREAM OF
LETTUCE SOUP

BROWN RICE, MUSHROOM
AND LENTIL SALAD

COURGETTE, PEPPER AND
TOMATO SALAD

SAUSAGE AND APPLE SLICE

COLD SPANISH OMELETTE

RICOTTA AND DILL WHOLEWHEAT FLAN

ALMOND SURPRISE CAKE

FRESH FRUIT

Most of the cooking and preparation for this menu can be done the day before. If Thermos flasks are unavailable for the Chilled cream of lettuce soup, reduce a little of the liquid in the preparation and add some ice cubes to the container to keep the soup chilled.

Both the salads 'travel' well as, unlike some salads, they benefit from being dressed in advance. Prepare them in rigid polythene containers ready for transportation.

The Sausage and apple slice and the Ricotta and dill wholewheat flan can be kept in an airtight tin or closely wrapped in foil.

CLOCKWISE FROM THE TOP:
*Brown rice, mushroom and lentil salad; Sausage
and apple slice; Chilled cream of lettuce soup;
Cold Spanish omelette (recipes page 82)*

Chilled Cream of Lettuce Soup

SERVES 6

25 g (1 oz) butter
1 lettuce
1 bunch spring onions,
*   chopped*
2 potatoes, peeled and diced
900 ml (1½ pints) chicken
*   stock*
salt
freshly ground black pepper

TO SERVE:

1 x 150 ml (5 fl oz) carton
*   single cream*
1 tablespoon chopped chives

PREPARTION TIME: *10 minutes*

COOKING TIME: *30 minutes*

1. Melt the butter in a pan, add the lettuce, spring onions and potatoes. Cover the pan and cook gently for 10 minutes, stirring frequently to prevent sticking.
2. Add the stock, salt and pepper. Bring to the boil and simmer for 20 minutes. Cool, then blend until smooth.
3. Chill well, then add the cream and garnish with chopped chives. (Pictured on page 81.)

Brown Rice, Mushroom and Lentil Salad

SERVES 6

100 g (4 oz) red lentils, soaked
*   for 1 hour*
100 g (4 oz) brown rice
6 tablespoons oil
2 tablespoons wine vinegar
salt
freshly ground black pepper
175 g (6 oz) mushrooms, sliced
1 small onion, peeled and
*   finely chopped*

PREPARATION TIME: *10 minutes,*
*   plus soaking*

COOKING TIME: *40 minutes*

1. Boil the lentils for 30 minutes in unsalted water.
2. Cook the rice in lightly salted water for 30-40 minutes until tender.
3. Mix together the oil, vinegar, salt and pepper and marinate the mushrooms and onion in the dressing.
4. Strain the lentils and rice, add to the mushrooms. Mix well. Leave to cool. (Pictured on page 80.)

Courgette, Pepper and Tomato Salad

SERVES 6

450 g (1 lb) small courgettes
225 g (8 oz) tomatoes, skinned
*   and quartered*
1 red pepper, cored, seeded and
*   diced*
1 green pepper, cored, seeded
*   and diced*
3 tablespoons oil
juice of 1 lemon
salt
freshly ground black pepper
2 teaspoons dried oregano

PREPARATION TIME: *15 minutes*

COOKING TIME: *5 minutes*

1. Slice the courgettes. Put them into a pan of lightly salted water. Bring to the boil, cook for 2-3 minutes, then strain and pour cold water over.
2. Put the courgettes in a large bowl, add the tomatoes and peppers.
3. Mix together the oil, lemon juice, salt, pepper and oregano. Pour on to the vegetables and toss lightly.

NOTE:
Fresh marjoram or chervil could replace the oregano.

Sausage and Apple Slice

SERVES 6

1 small onion, peeled and
*   chopped*
1 tablespoon oil
450 g (1 lb) sausage meat
1 teaspoon mixed herbs
salt
freshly ground black pepper
1 egg, beaten
1 x 375 g (13 oz) packet puff
*   pastry, thawed*
1 small cooking apple, peeled,
*   cored and sliced*

PREPARATION TIME: *25 minutes,*
*   plus chilling*

COOKING TIME: *35-50 minutes*

OVEN: *220°C, 425°F, Gas Mark 7;*
*   180°C, 350°F, Gas Mark 4*

This recipe is equally good served as a hot meal with vegetables, or try it cut into fingers for a party instead of the usual sausage rolls.

1. Fry the onion in the oil until soft, cool slightly, then add the sausage meat with the herbs, salt, pepper and half the egg.
2. Roll out three-quarters of the pastry to a 25 cm (10 inch) square. Place on a greased baking sheet.
3. Spread the sausage meat over the pastry to within 1 cm (½ inch) of the edge. Put the apple slices on top of the sausage meat. Dampen the edges with water.
4. Roll out the remaining pastry. Cut into 1 cm (½ inch) wide strips and make into a woven trellis over the top of the apples. Brush with the remaining egg and chill for 30 minutes.
5. Place in a preheated oven for 15 minutes. Reduce the oven temperature and cook for a further 15-30 minutes. Serve cold. (Pictured on page 81.)

Cold Spanish Omelette

SERVES 6

2 tablespoons oil
1 small onion, peeled and
*   chopped*
1 small red pepper, cored,
*   seeded and sliced*
2 cooked potatoes, diced
6 eggs, beaten
50 g (2 oz) Spanish sausage,
*   sliced*
salt
freshly ground black pepper

PREPARATION TIME: *5 minutes*

COOKING TIME: *10 minutes*

Spanish sausage or Chorizo is quite hot and spicy. It is available from larger supermarkets and delicatessens. If it is unavailable, salami or garlic sausage can be used instead.

1. In a pan put 1 tablespoon of the oil and gently fry the onion, peppers and potatoes until lightly browned.
2. Cool slightly, then add to the eggs with the sausage, salt and pepper.
3. Put the remaining oil in a large omelette pan, heat gently, pour in the egg mixture and cook until the egg has set on the bottom of the pan.
4. Turn the omelette out on to a plate, then slide back into the pan and cook the other side. Cool, then cut into wedges. (Pictured on page 80.)

VARIATION:
A delicious alternative to this recipe can be made by substituting the potatoes and peppers with 100 g (4 oz) courgettes and 50 g (2 oz) mushrooms.

Courgette, pepper and tomato salad; Ricotta and dill wholewheat flan; Almond surprise cake

Ricotta and Dill Wholewheat Flan

SERVES 6

75 g (3 oz) wholewheat flour
75 g (3 oz) self-raising flour,
*   sifted*
75 g (3 oz) white cooking fat or
*   lard*
water, to mix

FILLING:

225 g (8 oz) ricotta cheese
1 tablespoon fresh dill,
*   chopped or 1½ teaspoons*
*   dried dill weed*
2 eggs, beaten
1 x 150 ml (5 fl oz) carton
*   single cream*
salt
freshly ground black pepper

PREPARATION TIME: *20 minutes,*
*   plus chilling*

COOKING TIME: *40 minutes*

OVEN: *200°C, 400°F, Gas Mark 6;*
*   180°C, 350°F, Gas Mark 4*

1. To make the pastry, mix together the wholewheat flour and self-raising flour. Rub in the fat until the mixture resembles breadcrumbs. Stir in 2-3 tablespoons water and mix to a soft dough. Chill the pastry for 30 minutes.
2. In a bowl mix together the ricotta, dill, eggs, cream, salt and pepper.
3. Roll out the pastry and use to line a 20 cm (8 inch) flan tin, then pour in the filling. Bake in a preheated oven for 20 minutes, then reduce the heat for a further 20 minutes. Serve cold.

VARIATION:
Ricotta is a soft Italian cheese. If unobtainable, it can be substituted with curd or sieved cottage cheese.

Almond Surprise Cake

SERVES 6

FILLING:

1 egg white
75 g (3 oz) ground almonds
75 g (3 oz) caster sugar
½ teaspoon almond essence

CAKE:

175 g (6 oz) butter
175 g (6 oz) caster sugar
1 teaspoon almond essence
2 eggs, plus 1 egg yolk, beaten
225 g (8 oz) self-raising flour,
*   sifted*
2-3 tablespoons milk
1 tablespoon flaked almonds

PREPARATION TIME: *20 minutes*

COOKING TIME: *1-1¼ hours*

OVEN: *180°C, 350°F, Gas Mark 4*

1. Grease and line a 1 kg (2 lb) loaf tin.
2. Make the filling by whisking the egg white until stiff, then add the ground almonds, sugar and almond essence. Roll into a sausage the same length as the tin.
3. Cream together the butter, sugar and almond essence until light and fluffy. Gradually beat in the eggs and yolk. Fold in the flour, adding a little milk if necessary to make a dropping consistency.
4. Put half the cake mixture into the tin. Place the almond filling on top, then cover with the remaining cake mixture.
5. Sprinkle with the flaked almonds. Bake in a preheated oven for 1-1¼ hours until springy when pressed. Turn out on to a wire tray to cool.

Autumn

The period between September and the end of November covers a large span of changing weather. September can often be a wonderful holiday month, especially if we are lucky enough to have an 'Indian summer', and then the next thing we know, we are muffled up in our winter clothes and thinking about Christmas!

FREEZING AND STORING

The month of September itself can be a very busy time for the cook. Those with freezers will still be picking and preparing their vegetables, and the more old-fashioned of us will be busy bottling late fruits. Plums are very reasonably priced during the early part of the month, and freeze well for pies and crumbles. Simply wash the fruits, split them and remove the stones, then pack in polythene bags with a little granulated sugar and freeze. Victorias freeze particularly well.

The picking of apples and pears for storage should be done most carefully, if you are lucky enough to have the trees in your garden. Each fruit to be stored must be in perfect condition, that is to say without bruises or blemishes of any kind. Wrap each one in old newspaper and pack carefully into cardboard or wooden boxes. Store in a cool place.

Any blemished fruit is best peeled, cored, sliced and mixed with a little sugar, then cooked over a low heat. Bramley apples tend to puff up to a purée, whereas other varieties will keep their shape. Pears should be gently stewed before freezing.

NUTS

Much of our countryside abounds in hazel nuts, cob nuts and chestnuts, and there is always a race to see if you can beat the squirrels before they strip the trees bare! If you can find enough nuts to pick it is well worthwhile storing some for Christmas. The hazel and cob nuts may be picked while still green, as long as they are mature enough to contain a nut. Make sure that each nut is perfect, then place them in an old biscuit tin and bury the tin under about one foot of soil. After two to three months the nuts will have ripened and will still be moist inside.

Chestnuts need different treatment. They should only be picked when the outer prickly shell has split open to reveal the brown nut. If picked too early, the nuts will not keep. One still has quite a job to remove the ripe nuts from the prickly casing, but I find the best method is to be armed with rubber gloves and two sharp stones to prize the casing apart. You can either store your chestnuts in a cool, damp place with plenty of ventilation or make chestnut purée or 'marron glacé' in preparation for Christmas. This all sounds like a great deal of work, but children enjoy taking part, especially if they have something to show for it at the end of the exercise!

PRESERVING

Early autumn is the time to make your apple and herb jellies and chutneys – especially green tomato chutney with those frustratingly unripened fruits. Fruits that have reached the correct size may be picked and placed in a warm dark place to ripen, or try splitting them and frying them – you will be pleasantly surprised! Use the smaller fruits for tomato chutneys or relishes. Bramble jelly is popular with most families, but first pick out the largest and least damaged, and open freeze them for later use with stewed apple for pies and crumbles, then the remaining fruits may be used for jams and jellies.

MUSHROOMS

You may also be lucky in finding field mushrooms and other edible fungi. French people are brought up to know what can or cannot be eaten, as some fungi can be poisonous. If you are interested in this subject, there are several books on the market describing what you can and cannot eat. If in doubt, do not eat them.

GAME

Game is in abundance during September, October and November, but is always expensive unless you happen to know a local farmer. Roast game or delicious game pies can be made during the autumn months.

FISH

Home-smoking of fish is very popular, and there are several different handy home smokers on the market. Fish prices are usually lower in the autumn, especially salmon, as this is the end of the season. Follow the manufacturer's instructions carefully and then the smoked fish can either be eaten immediately or well packed and frozen for Christmas.

CHRISTMAS BAKING

Christmas cakes and puddings are best made in October. A little brandy or rum incorporated into these will help them keep. Store puddings with their covers left on in a cool place, and Christmas cakes in a well sealed tin. For a really moist cake, make holes with a knitting needle in the base of the cake and pour in a little extra brandy or rum. If you do this two or three times before icing the cake in December, it will be moist and delicious.

THE MENUS

November is a month when you can enjoy the fruits of your labours, eating summer vegetables from your freezer and enjoying your home-bottled fruit and jams. Bonfire night is always an exciting occasion for the children, and there is a special menu for this celebration, planned for the enjoyment of grown-ups and children alike. Many of the recipes can be made in advance and frozen, to make less work on the day.

Lunch or Supper

(SEPTEMBER)

NUTTY STUFFED TOMATOES

COURGETTE AND BACON BAKE

HOT CRUSTY BREAD

MIXED SALAD VINAIGRETTE

BLACKBERRY AND APPLE MOUNTAIN

Nutty Stuffed Tomatoes

SERVES 6

6 large tomatoes
225 g (8 oz) cottage cheese
75 g (3 oz) salted peanuts,
  roughly chopped
1 tablespoon chopped basil
50 g (2 oz) sultanas
3 spring onions, finely chopped
salt
freshly ground black pepper
lettuce leaves, to serve

PREPARATION TIME: *30 minutes*

This recipe is delicious if made with the large nobbly Mediterranean tomatoes.

1. Cut the tops off the tomatoes and set aside. Hollow out the tomatoes, discarding the flesh and pips (these could be added to your stock pot).
2. Turn the cottage cheese into a bowl and add the peanuts, basil, sultanas and spring onions. Stir together until well mixed, then season to taste with salt and pepper.
3. Use this mixture to fill the tomato shells, then replace the caps.
4. Serve on individual plates, garnished with lettuce leaves.

Courgette and Bacon Bake

SERVES 6

1 kg (2 lb) small, firm
   courgettes, sliced into rings
4 whole eggs
450 ml (¾ pint) milk
200 g (7 oz) strong Cheddar
   cheese, grated
salt
freshly ground black pepper
pinch of paprika
75 g (3 oz) streaky bacon,
   lightly grilled

TO SERVE:
hot crusty bread
mixed salad with vinaigrette
   dressing

PREPARATION TIME: *30 minutes*
COOKING TIME: *about 1 hour*
OVEN: *180°C, 350°F, Gas Mark 4*

Home gardeners and
greengrocers' shops usually
have an abundance of
courgettes at this time of year.
They do not freeze
successfully by the usual
simple blanching method
since they have a very large
water content. If you wish to
freeze them they are best
used as ingredients for soups,
stews, ratatouille, etc.

1. Blanch the courgettes in
boiling water for 2 minutes,
then drain them in a colander
and allow to cool.
2. Beat together the eggs and
milk and stir in 150 g (5 oz) of
the cheese. Add salt, pepper
and paprika.
3. Lightly butter a 1.2 litre (2
pint) gratin dish and layer the
courgettes and bacon to
within 1 cm (½ inch) of the
top of the dish.
4. Pour over the egg mixture
and sprinkle with the
remaining cheese.
5. Bake in a preheated oven
for 40-45 minutes until set
and golden brown on top.
Serve with hot crusty bread
and a mixed salad in
vinaigrette.

Blackberry and Apple Mountain

SERVES 6

SPONGE:
50 g (2 oz) butter
50 g (2 oz) caster sugar
2 eggs, beaten
50 g (2 oz) self-raising flour,
   sifted

TOPPING:
750 g (1½ lb) Bramley cooking
   apples
4 tablespoons water
225 g (8 oz) fresh or frozen
   blackberries
sugar to taste
300 ml (½ pint) double or
   whipping cream, lightly
   whipped
25 g (1 oz) flaked almonds,
   toasted

PREPARATION TIME: *1¼ hours*
COOKING TIME: *25 minutes*
OVEN: *190°C, 375°C, Gas Mark 5*

1. To make the sponge,
lightly grease an 18 cm
(7 inch) sponge tin.
2. Cream the butter with the
sugar until light and fluffy.
Gradually beat in the eggs,
adding a little of the flour
from time to time to prevent
the mixture from curdling.
When all the egg is
incorporated gently stir in
the remaining flour.
3. Turn the mixture into the
prepared tin and cook in a
preheated oven for
approximately 25 minutes.
To test whether the cake is
cooked, gently make an
indentation with your finger
in the centre. If the mixture
springs back into place the
cake is ready. Remove from
the oven, turn out and allow
to cool on a wire tray.
4. Meanwhile, peel, core and

chop the apples and place
them in a saucepan. Add the
water, and cook over a gentle
heat, stirring occasionally,
until they become fluffy. Add
the blackberries and sugar to
taste, let them heat through
and then leave until cold.
5. To assemble the
mountain, place the sponge
on a serving plate, and pile
the apple and blackberry
mixture on top, forming a
cone shape. Spoon the
whipped cream over the top
and sprinkle with toasted
almonds.

NOTE:
Canned fruit is not suitable
for this dish. If gathering wild
fruit, pick from bushes
situated away from traffic, so
that you know it has not been
soiled by car fumes.

Evening Meal

SEPTEMBER

GARLIC AND PARSLEY
BAKED FIELD MUSHROOMS

HOT FRENCH BREAD

VEAL OLIVES

BUTTERED BROCCOLI

CREAMED POTATOES

PEARS IN GRENADINE

Garlic and Parsley Baked Field Mushrooms

SERVES 6

*450 g (1 lb) field mushrooms,
    stalks removed, then sliced
2 cloves garlic, crushed
75 g (3 oz) butter, melted
2 tablespoons chopped parsley
6 tablespoons double cream
salt
freshly ground black pepper*

PREPARATION TIME: *20 minutes*

COOKING TIME: *15-20 minutes*

OVEN: *200°C, 400°F, Gas Mark 6*

Carefully pick over wild mushrooms for any sign of termites. Discard these. If in any doubt, don't pick them.

1. Lightly grease 6 individual flameproof dishes, or one 600 ml (1 pint) gratin dish.
2. Arrange the sliced mushrooms in the dish or dishes.
3. Add the crushed garlic to the butter and stir to incorporate. Pour over the mushrooms.
4. Mix together the parsley, cream, salt and pepper, and pour over the buttered mushrooms.
5. Bake in a preheated oven for 10 minutes for individual dishes or 15-20 minutes for the large dish.
6. Serve hot, with hot French bread to soak up the juices.

Veal Olives

SERVES 6

6 x 100 g (4 oz) escalopes of
  veal

STUFFING:
175 g (6 oz) white
  breadcrumbs
225 g (8 oz) streaky bacon,
  finely chopped
100 g (4 oz) chicken livers,
  minced
1 medium onion, peeled and
  finely chopped
1 teaspoon dried tarragon
salt
freshly ground black pepper
1 egg, beaten

SAUCE:
100 g (4 oz) butter
2 tablespoons oil
100 g (4 oz) baby onions or
  shallots, peeled and chopped
600 ml (1 pint) stock
salt
freshly ground black pepper
40 g (1½ oz) cornflour
2 tablespoons water
300 ml (½ pint) single cream
2 tablespoons chopped fresh
  parsley

TO GARNISH:
lemon wedges
paprika pepper, for sprinkling

PREPARATION TIME: *30 minutes*
COOKING TIME: *1¼ hours*
OVEN: *180°C, 350°F, Gas Mark 4*

This recipe is a delicious
variation on the classic beef
olive.

1. Place the veal escalopes
between 2 pieces of
greaseproof paper, and beat
them with a rolling pin until
flat. Set aside while making
the stuffing.
2. Mix together the
breadcrumbs, bacon,
chicken livers, onion,
tarragon, salt and pepper,
and bind with the beaten egg.
3. Divide the mixture
between the escalopes, roll
up each one and secure with
cocktail sticks or string.

4. Heat the butter and oil in a
saucepan, and fry the olives
until gently browned on all
sides. Remove them from the
pan and place in a large
flameproof dish.
5. Toss the onions in the pan
juices, until lightly browned
and pour over the olives. Add
the stock, salt and pepper.
Cook in a preheated oven for
50 minutes.
6. Arrange the veal olives on
a serving dish and keep
warm.
7. Mix the cornflour with the
water and stir into the pan
juices. Place over the heat and
allow the sauce to come
gently to the boil, stirring as it
thickens. Simmer for 2-3
minutes, then remove from
the heat and stir in the cream
and parsley.
8. Pour the sauce over the
olives, sprinkle with paprika
pepper and garnish with
lemon wedges. Serve
immediately. Buttered
broccoli and creamed
potatoes go well with this
dish.

Pears in Grenadine

SERVES 6

6 firm pears, peeled and left
  whole
450 ml (¾ pint) grenadine
  syrup
750 ml (1¼ pints) water
1 teaspoon ground cloves
1 teaspoon ground cinnamon
1 teaspoon ground nutmeg
juice of 1 lemon
225 g (8 oz) sugar

TO SERVE:
vanilla ice cream or double or
  whipping cream, lightly
  whipped

PREPARATION TIME: *30 minutes*
COOKING TIME: *40 minutes, plus
  overnight soaking*

Grenadine is a syrup made of
pomegranates. It is
non-alcoholic, and you will
find that it is stocked by good
quality drink shops and
grocers. It is generally used
as a base for cocktails – the
best known of these being
Tequila Sunrise. It is rich red
in colour and gives a rich hue
to the pears.

1. Place the peeled pears in a
saucepan large enough for
them all to rest on the base.
Mix together the grenadine
and water and pour over the
pears.
2. Add the cloves, cinnamon,
nutmeg and lemon juice,
then bring slowly to the boil.
Simmer for 2-3 minutes, then
remove from the heat and
leave overnight to allow the
pears to soak up the
marinade.
3. Remove the pears and
arrange on a serving dish.
4. Strain the marinade into a
clean saucepan, and cook
rapidly until the liquid has
reduced by half.
5. Add the sugar and stir
over a gentle heat until
dissolved, then boil again
until a syrup is obtained. (A
sugar thermometer should
register 107°C, 225°F or the
syrup will form a fine, thin
thread if allowed to fall from
a spoon on to a dish.)
6. Cool the syrup and pour
over the pears. Allow to cool
before serving with ice cream
or cream.

Dinner Party
SEPTEMBER

CHINESE STUFFED AVOCADO PEARS

BROWN BREAD AND BUTTER

TOURNEDOS EN CROÛTE

CHEESY LAYERED POTATOES

FRENCH BEANS TOSSED
IN BUTTER AND GARLIC

SCOTTISH RASPBERRY MERINGUE NESTS

Chinese Stuffed Avocado Pears

SERVES 6

3 ripe avocados
1 small lemon wedge

FILLING:

1 x 200 g (7 oz) can tuna fish,
drained and flaked
75 g (3 oz) bean sprouts,
chopped
1 medium carrot, peeled and
grated
1 tablespoon chopped fresh
parsley
1 stick celery, finely chopped
pinch of ground ginger
pinch of sugar
3 tablespoons mayonnaise
salt
freshly ground black pepper
sprigs of parsley, to garnish
thinly sliced brown bread and
butter, to serve

PREPARATION TIME: *30 minutes*

1. Carefully halve the avocados, remove the stones, and wipe the cut surface with lemon juice.
2. Mix all the filling ingredients together and divide the mixture between the halves of avocado.
3. Serve on individual plates garnished with sprigs of parsley. Arrange the brown bread and butter on a separate plate.

NOTE:
There are basically 3 varieties of avocado. Firstly the classic pear-shaped ones, then the very shiny green 'rugger ball' shaped ones and lastly the small knobbly ones. These are *not* ripe when green – you must wait until the skin is almost black.

Tournedos en Croûte

SERVES 6

6 x 100 g (4 oz) fillet steaks
25 g (1 oz) butter
1 medium onion, peeled and
    finely chopped
175 g (6 oz) button
    mushrooms, finely chopped
1 tablespoon chopped fresh
    parsley
salt
freshly ground black pepper
1 x 375 g (13 oz) packet puff
    pastry
100 g (4 oz) smooth pâté
1 egg, beaten

PREPARATION TIME: *30 minutes*

COOKING TIME: *30 minutes*

OVEN: *220°C, 425°F, Gas Mark 7*

Buy fillets that are small in
diameter and at least 2.5 cm
(1 inch) thick.

1. Trim any fat or sinew from
the steaks. Melt the butter in a
frying pan, and gently fry the
steaks on either side to seal in
the juices. Remove from the
pan and set aside to cool.
2. Add the onion and
mushrooms to the pan and
cook over a gentle heat until
the onion is soft. Stir in the
chopped parsley, salt and
pepper. Allow to cool.
3. Roll out the pastry to
approximately 36 cm (14
inches) square, and divide
into 6 equal parts.
4. Place a little of the onion
mixture in the centre of each
piece of pastry. Spread each
steak with pâté and place
pâté-side down on the pastry.
5. Gently bring up the edges,
trimming off any excess
pastry, and seal with beaten
egg, making sure that there
are no holes in the pastry,
otherwise the juices will run
during cooking.
6. Lightly grease a baking
sheet, turn the steaks over,
and place on the sheet. Use
the pastry trimmings to make
leaves for decoration. Brush
the pastry with beaten egg
and cook in a preheated oven
for 15 minutes, or until risen
and golden brown in colour.
Serve immediately with
Cheesy layered potatoes (see
right) and French beans
tossed in butter and garlic.

Cheesy Layered Potatoes

SERVES 6

750 g (1½ lb) potatoes, peeled
    and thinly sliced
50 g (2 oz) butter, softened
3 pinches of ground nutmeg
salt
freshly ground black pepper
100 g (4 oz) Cheddar cheese,
    grated
450 ml (¾ pint) milk
1 x 150 ml (¼ pint) carton
    single cream

PREPARATION TIME: *30 minutes*

COOKING TIME: *1½ hours*

OVEN: *180°C, 350°F, Gas Mark 4*

1. Butter a 1.2 litre (2 pint)
gratin dish, and cover the
base with a layer of
overlapping potato slices.
Dot with butter, sprinkle with
a little nutmeg, salt, pepper
and cheese. Repeat these
layers until the ingredients
are used up, finishing with a
layer of cheese.
2. Mix together the milk and
cream and pour into the dish,
taking care not to disturb the
cheese.
3. Cook in a preheated oven
for 1½ hours, or until the
potatoes are tender and the
topping browned.

Scottish Raspberry Meringue Nests

SERVES 6

120 ml (4 fl oz) egg whites
225 g (8 oz) caster sugar

FILLING:

350 g (12 oz) raspberries,
    hulled
175 ml (6 fl oz) double or
    whipping cream, whipped
25 g (1 oz) blanched almonds,
    chopped

PREPARATION TIME: *40 minutes*

COOKING TIME: *1½-2 hours*

OVEN: *110°C, 225°F, Gas Mark ¼*

Raspberries are available
from June until September,
although the English main
crop comes in July. A
different variety of raspberry
is grown in Scotland, and
these are available in the
shops during September.

1. Whisk the egg whites until
very stiff, then add 1
tablespoon of the sugar and
beat this well in. Using a
metal spoon or spatula,
carefully fold in the
remaining sugar.
2. Lightly oil a baking sheet,
then place a sheet of
greaseproof or non-stick
silicone paper over. Lightly
oil the top of the greaseproof
paper, if using.
3. Spoon the meringue into
a large forcing bag fitted with
a plain 1 cm (½ inch) tube.
Pipe 10 cm (4 inch) circles on
to the paper, then pipe round
the edge of each circle to
form the nest shape.
4. Place the nests in a
preheated oven for 1½-2
hours, or until they peel away
from the paper. Cool on a
wire tray. The nests may be
made in advance and stored
in a tin or polythene
container.
5. When ready for use,
divide the raspberries
between the nests. Place the
whipped cream in a piping
bag fitted with a star nozzle
and pipe whirls of cream on
the top of each. Sprinkle with
the almonds.

CONSOMMÉ

RILLETTES DE PORC

HERB BREAD

AUTUMN SPINACH SALAD

SELECTION OF FRESH FRUIT
AND CHEESE

Herb Bread

SERVES 6

100 g (4 oz) butter, creamed
2 tablespoons chopped fresh
*   parsley*
1 tablespoon fresh or dried sage
1 tablespoon fresh or dried dill
*   weed*
salt
freshly ground black pepper
1 French stick loaf

PREPARATION TIME: *20 minutes*

COOKING TIME: *15 minutes*

OVEN: *190°C, 375°F, Gas Mark 5*

1. Place the creamed butter in a mixing bowl and add all the herbs and seasonings. Cut the loaf at 2.5 cm (1 inch) intervals almost to the base.
2. Spread the herb butter between each slice and re-form the loaf.
3. Place the loaf on a large piece of aluminium foil, gently bring up the sides and ends and seal them carefully so as not to lose any juices during cooking. This may be done in advance.
4. When almost ready to serve, place the loaf in a preheated oven for 15 minutes.
5. Remove from the foil and serve.

Rillettes de Porc

SERVES 6

1½ kg (3 lb) belly of pork on
*   the bone*
750 g (1½ lb) pork bones
2 sage leaves
bouquet garni
salt
freshly ground black pepper

TO SERVE:
shredded lettuce (optional)
tomato slices (optional)
cucumber slices (optional)

PREPARATION TIME: *20 minutes,*
*   plus setting*

COOKING TIME: *3 hours*

Rillettes are a form of potted meat, and they are a great speciality of the Loire region of France. Each town in the area has its own methods of making this dish, often using goose or rabbit to complement the pork. The following recipe is a simple but delicious version, relatively inexpensive to prepare. The Rillettes take a while to cook and set but can be made in advance. They will keep in the refrigerator for at least a week.

1. Place the pork, pork bones, sage leaves and bouquet garni in a large saucepan. Add just enough water to cover, with a little salt and pepper.
2. Cook over a gentle heat until the water has almost evaporated and the meat is literally falling off the bone.
3. Strain off the remaining juices, much of which will be pork fat.
4. Remove all the meat from the bones and place in a mixing bowl, discarding the sage and bouquet garni. Using 2 forks, shred the meat finely and check the seasoning.
5. Place the meat in a terrine or 6 small ramekin dishes. The dishes should only be three-quarters full.
6. Strain the juices over the meat, and allow to set in the refrigerator for at least 3 hours before serving.
7. Serve (if liked) on a bed of shredded lettuce with tomato and cucumber slices and accompany with the Herb bread and Autumn spinach salad (see right).

Autumn Spinach Salad

SERVES 6

25 g (1 oz) butter
100 g (4 oz) streaky bacon,
*   finely chopped*
50 g (2 oz) blanched almonds,
*   chopped*
1 bunch spring onions, sliced
*   into rings*
350 g (12 oz) fresh spinach,
*   washed and roughly*
*   shredded*
2 eggs, hard-boiled and
*   chopped*
50 g (2 oz) currants

DRESSING:
3 tablespoons olive oil
2 tablespoons white wine
*   vinegar*
1 clove garlic, peeled and
*   crushed*
1 teaspoon runny honey
1 tablespoon single cream
salt
freshly ground black pepper

PREPARATION TIME: *30 minutes*

COOKING TIME: *10 minutes*

1. Melt the butter in a frying pan, and add the bacon, almonds and spring onions. Fry gently until crisp.
2. Place the spinach in a salad bowl, and mix in the chopped egg and currants.
3. Mix all the dressing ingredients and pour into the saucepan. Stir well, then pour this warm mixture over the spinach, and toss together. Serve at once.

VARIATION:
The spinach really makes this salad, but if the weather has been bad and you are unable to obtain good fresh spinach, use a finely shredded white cabbage as an alternative.

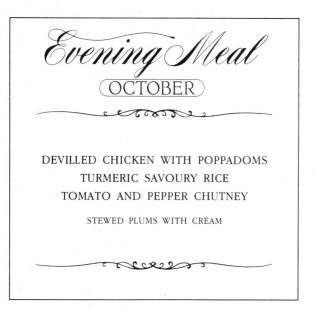

Evening Meal
(OCTOBER)

DEVILLED CHICKEN WITH POPPADOMS
TURMERIC SAVOURY RICE
TOMATO AND PEPPER CHUTNEY

STEWED PLUMS WITH CREAM

Devilled Chicken

SERVES 6

1 x 750 g (3½ lb) fresh chicken
75 g (3 oz) butter, melted
2 tablespoons oil
2 onions, peeled and sliced
600 ml (1 pint) stock
1 tablespoon chutney
2 teaspoons made English
  mustard
1 teaspoon anchovy essence
pinch of cayenne
salt
freshly ground black pepper

TO SERVE:
Turmeric savoury rice (see
  next page)
poppadoms

PREPARATION TIME:	*20 minutes*
COOKING TIME:	*2 hours*
OVEN:	*160°C, 325°F, Gas Mark 3*

This dish has a fairly mild taste, the quantity of mustard can be doubled if preferred.

1. Gently fry the chicken on all sides in the butter and oil in a large frying pan. Remove from the pan and place in a large flameproof dish.
2. Lightly fry the onions in the pan juices, then add the remaining ingredients.
3. Pour this mixture over the chicken, cover, and place in a preheated oven for 1½ hours or until the chicken is cooked.
4. Remove the chicken from the pot, place on a serving dish and keep warm.
5. Allow the juices to stand for a few minutes, then skim off any fat with a large cooking spoon, and pour the juices over the chicken.
6. Serve with poppadoms, Turmeric savoury rice and Tomato and pepper chutney (see next page).

Poppadoms

Many people find cooking poppadoms very difficult. The usual faults lie in not getting the oil hot enough, and not working quickly enough. Asian shops sell a variety of different flavours.

Take a good-sized frying pan and pour in cooking oil to a depth of 3 mm (⅛ inch). It may be necessary to add more oil if you are cooking more than 6 poppadoms, as they tend to soak up a certain amount when cooking. Heat the oil until you can see a little blue smoke rising from it, then put in the first poppadom. Flatten it immediately with an egg flip to prevent it from curling up too much.

Immediately turn over and cook the other side, then remove to a piece of kitchen paper to soak up the excess oil. Each poppadom should only take 2 seconds per side to cook. Take care that the oil does not overheat as this can be a dangerous fire hazard, especially if you are using gas.

Cooked in this way, the poppadoms will be very crispy, and will retain their crispness for at least an hour if kept gently warmed.

To serve, pile them up on a large serving platter or tray.

Turmeric Savoury Rice

SERVES 6

350 g (12 oz) long-grain rice
225 g (8 oz) French beans, cut into 1 cm (½ inch) lengths
1 red pepper, diced
1 green pepper, diced
1 x 425 g (15 oz) can red kidney beans, drained
1 x 325 g (11½ oz) can sweetcorn kernels, drained
2 tablespoons turmeric
salt
freshly ground black pepper

PREPARATION TIME: *20 minutes*

COOKING TIME: *about 30 minutes*

OVEN: *150°C, 300°F, Gas Mark 2*

1. Cook the rice in boiling, salted water until just tender. Drain and place in a large mixing bowl. Cover if cooking in advance.
2. Blanch the fresh beans and peppers in boiling, salted water and drain.
3. Add the beans, peppers, kidney beans, sweetcorn and turmeric to the rice. Add plenty of salt and pepper.
4. Place the savoury rice in a buttered flameproof dish, and cover with foil. Place in a preheated oven, stirring gently from time to time to heat through evenly, about 10 minutes (30-45 minutes if reheating from cold).

Tomato and Pepper Chutney

SERVES 12

450 g (1 lb) tomatoes, skinned and roughly chopped
2 green peppers, cored, seeded and cut into slices
3 medium onions, peeled and chopped
100 g (4 oz) seedless raisins
pinch of ginger
1 tablespoon coriander seeds ⎫ *tied*
12 cloves ⎬ *in a muslin*
4 dried chillies ⎭ *bag*
225 g (8 oz) demerara sugar
600 ml (1 pint) wine vinegar

PREPARATION TIME: *30 minutes*

COOKING TIME: *approximately 2 hours*

1. Place all the ingredients in a pan and simmer gently until the mixture has thickened.
2. When the correct consistency is obtained, remove the muslin bag, pour the chutney into hot sterilized jars and seal.

NOTE:
For maximum flavour this chutney should be made in advance and kept for 2 weeks before eating. It will store for up to 6 months.

Dinner Party

OCTOBER

SCALLOPS NANTUA

FINGERS OF TOAST

BRAISED TURKEY BREASTS
WITH CHESTNUTS

LEEKS WITH MARJORAM SAUCE

CHEESY DUCHESSE POTATOES

CREAMY APPLE RING MOULD
WITH SWEET MINT SAUCE

Scallops Nantua

SERVES 6

225 g (8 oz) freshwater crayfish
   or prawns in their shells
450 ml (¾ pint) water
1 slice onion
3 slices carrot
1 bay leaf
12 scallops
25 g (1 oz) butter
25 g (1 oz) flour
2 tablespoons double cream
salt
freshly ground black pepper

TOPPING:
50 g (2 oz) butter
75 g (3 oz) breadcrumbs

TO GARNISH:
sprigs of parsley (optional)

PREPARATION TIME: *30 minutes*

COOKING TIME: *30 minutes*

1. Place the crayfish or prawns in a saucepan and pour in the water. Add the onion, carrot and bay leaf. Bring to the boil, and continue boiling rapidly until the liquid has reduced by approximately one-third.
2. Reduce the heat and add the scallops. Simmer gently for 10 minutes. If the scallops are cooked too quickly they tend to become rubbery in texture.
3. Strain off the liquid and set it aside.
4. Separate the scallops and cut each one into 4. Set aside.
5. Peel the crayfish or prawns and pass through a liquidizer or food processor together with 300 ml (½ pint) of the fish liquor.
6. To make the sauce, melt the butter in a saucepan, add the flour and cook the roux for 2-3 minutes. Remove from the heat and gently stir in the fish purée. When all is incorporated return to the heat and bring slowly to the boil.
7. Stir in the cream and the scallops, and add salt and pepper.
8. Divide the mixture between 6 deep scallop shells, or individual ovenproof dishes.
9. To make the topping, melt the butter and stir in the breadcrumbs. Sprinkle over the top of each dish, and gently brown under the grill. Serve garnished with sprigs of parsley, if using, accompanied by fingers of toast.

Braised Turkey Breasts with Chestnuts

SERVES 6

50 g (2 oz) butter
2 tablespoons oil
500 g (1¼ lb) turkey breasts,
*   skinned and sliced*
2 medium onions, peeled and
*   chopped*
100 g (4 oz) streaky bacon,
*   rinded and diced*
1 tablespoon plain flour
300 ml (½ pint) chicken stock
150 ml (¼ pint) white wine
1 teaspoon dried tarragon
1 x 450 g (1 lb) can whole
*   chestnuts, drained*
3 tablespoons double cream
salt
freshly ground black pepper

PREPARATION TIME: *20 minutes*

COOKING TIME: *30 minutes*

1. Melt the butter and oil in a large heavy frying pan. Fry the turkey breasts for 2 minutes either side, until lightly browned. Remove them from the pan.
2. Add the onions and bacon to the pan juices, and fry gently, stirring, for 5 minutes.
3. Sprinkle in the flour and cook, stirring, for 1 minute. Gradually add the stock to the pan, stirring gently until well incorporated. Add the wine, tarragon and chestnuts.
4. Return the fillets to the pan, making sure that they are well covered with sauce. Cook gently for 20 minutes, stirring occasionally.
5. Remove the turkey fillets, arrange them on a serving dish and keep warm.
6. Add the cream to the sauce with a little salt and pepper. Take care not to add too much salt, as the bacon gives a salty taste to the dish.
7. Pour the sauce over the turkey fillets and serve.
8. Leeks with marjoram sauce and Cheesy duchesse potatoes (see below) go well with this dish.

NOTE:
Turkey breasts can now be obtained from most large supermarkets. They are sometimes ready sliced, but normally they are packed as the whole breast, and need to be cut horizontally to form thin fillets.

Cheesy Duchesse Potatoes

SERVES 6

1 kg (2 lb) potatoes, peeled
50 g (2 oz) butter, softened
3 egg yolks
50 g (2 oz) grated Cheddar
*   cheese*
pinch of ground nutmeg
salt
freshly ground black pepper
beaten egg, to glaze

PREPARATION TIME: *20 minutes*

COOKING TIME: *40 minutes*

OVEN: *190°C, 375°F, Gas Mark 5*

1. Cut the potatoes into even-sized pieces and boil them gently in salted water until tender. Drain them in a colander, and allow to stand for 3-4 minutes until the steam subsides. This ensures that they will be dry and fluffy.
2. Place the potatoes in a mixing bowl and mash with a potato masher.
3. When there are no lumps to be seen, beat in the butter, yolks, cheese, nutmeg, salt and pepper.
4. Grease a large baking sheet and place the potato mixture in a large forcing bag fitted with a rose piping tube. Pipe out into cone shapes on to the prepared baking sheet and bake in a preheated oven for 10 minutes.
5. Remove the potatoes from the oven, brush with beaten egg, and return them to the oven to brown.

Leeks with Marjoram Sauce

SERVES 6

6 medium leeks, washed and
*   cut into rings*

SAUCE:
3 egg yolks
juice of 1 lemon
225 g (8 oz) butter, melted and
*   cooled*
1 tablespoon fresh or dried
*   marjoram*
salt
freshly ground black pepper

PREPARATION TIME: *20 minutes*

COOKING TIME: *15 minutes*

1. Cook the leeks in boiling salted water, drain and keep warm while making the sauce.
2. Place the yolks and lemon juice in a heavy pan, preferably cast iron. Whisk together over a very gentle heat until the mixture is thick and frothy. Do not let it boil or it will curdle.
3. Remove from the heat, and very gradually beat in the melted butter (this can be done in the liquidizer or food processor).
4. When all the butter is incorporated, add the marjoram, salt and pepper.
5. Place the leeks in a serving dish and pour over the sauce.

Creamy Apple Ring Mould

SERVES 6

3 large apples, peeled, cored and sliced
150 ml (¼ pint) water
rind and juice of 1 lemon
20 g (¾ oz) powdered gelatine
2 eggs
2 egg yolks
50 g (2 oz) caster sugar
1 x 150 ml (5 fl oz) carton double or whipping cream, whipped
Sweet Mint Sauce (see right), to serve

PREPARATION TIME: *30 minutes, plus setting*

COOKING TIME: *20 minutes*

Bramley apples are best, alternatively use Blenheims, Grenadiers or Howgates.

1. Place the apples in a pan with the water and lemon rind. Cover and stew gently until the apples are cooked. Set aside to cool. Soften the gelatine in the lemon juice and add to the apples.
2. Place the eggs, egg yolks and sugar in a mixing bowl and whisk them over a pan of gently simmering water until white and thick.
3. Stir in the cooled apple, then fold in the cream and turn into a wetted 1 litre (1¾ pint) ring mould. Chill until set.
4. When ready to serve, turn out the apple ring on to a serving platter and drizzle the Sweet mint sauce (see right) over the top.

Sweet Mint Sauce

SERVES 6

175 g (6 oz) caster sugar
300 ml (½ pint) water
2 tablespoons fresh or dried mint

PREPARATION TIME: *10 minutes*

COOKING TIME: *8-10 minutes*

A sweet and tangy sauce which contrasts well with the creamy apple taste.

1. Place all the ingredients together in a pan, and stir gently over the heat until the sugar has dissolved. Raise the heat and boil until a light syrup is obtained.
2. Allow to cool, then pour over the Creamy apple ring just before serving.

NOTE:
If growing your own mint, the nicest varieties for this recipe are apple mint or peppermint. To dry your own mint, pick it at its very best between August and September. Tie it together in bunches with string and hang it up in a warm, dry place.

Lunch or Supper

NOVEMBER

CREAM OF ARTICHOKE SOUP
PARMESAN CROÛTONS

SEAFOOD FLAN
BUTTERED LEAF SPINACH

DRIED FRUIT AND SPICE COMPÔTE

Cream of Artichoke Soup with Parmesan Croûtons

SERVES 6

50 g (2 oz) butter
450 g (1 lb) Jerusalem
  artichokes, peeled and sliced
450 g (1 lb) potatoes, peeled
  and sliced
2 medium onions, peeled and
  sliced
600 ml (1 pint) milk
300 ml (½ pint) chicken stock
salt
freshly ground black pepper
1 x 150 ml (5 fl oz) carton
  single cream

PARMESAN CROÛTONS:

3 thick slices white bread,
  crusts removed, cut into 1 cm
  (½ inch) squares
oil, for frying
1 tablespoon grated Parmesan
  cheese

PREPARATION TIME: *30 minutes*

COOKING TIME: *about 1¼ hours*

Jerusalem artichokes need a great deal of patience to peel and prepare but the job is well worth while as the finished soup is really delicious, especially when served with the Parmesan croûtons.

1. Melt the butter in a large heavy saucepan, and add the artichokes, potatoes and onions. Stir well to coat all the vegetables, then cover. Cook for 20-25 minutes over a gentle heat, so that the vegetables sweat in the butter, but do not brown. Toss the pan from time to time to ensure even cooking.
2. Remove the lid from the pan and add the milk, chicken stock, salt and freshly ground black pepper.
3. Allow the soup to simmer for 45 minutes, stirring from time to time.
4. Cool the soup a little then pass through a liquidizer, food processor or fine sieve. The use of an electric machine will result in a much creamier soup.
5. Serve in individual bowls with a swirl of cream to garnish, and Parmesan croûtons.
6. To make the croûtons, fry the cubes of bread in hot oil, turning all the time, about 5 minutes. Drain on paper towels and toss in the grated Parmesan while still hot.

Seafood Flan

SERVES 6

1 x 375 g (13 oz) packet frozen
  shortcrust pastry, thawed

FILLING:
50 g (2 oz) butter
1 bunch spring onions,
  trimmed and sliced
1 x 185 g (6½ oz) can
  crabmeat
225 g (8 oz) shelled prawns
2 tablespoons dry white wine
3 eggs
1 egg yolk
150 ml (¼ pint) single cream
1 tablespoon tomato purée
salt
freshly ground black pepper
25 g (1 oz) Gruyère cheese,
  grated

PREPARATION TIME: *30 minutes*

COOKING TIME: *40-50 minutes*

OVEN: *180°C, 350°F, Gas Mark 4;*
  160°C, 325°F, Gas Mark 3

For a cheaper dish, replace
the shellfish with white fish
and canned shrimps.

1. Roll out the pastry and use
to line a 20 cm (8 inch) flan
dish. Bake blind in a
preheated oven for 15-20
minutes.
2. Meanwhile make up the
filling. Melt the butter in a
saucepan and add the spring
onions. Cook gently for 5-7
minutes, but do not allow the
onions to brown.
3. Add the crabmeat and
prawns and cook for a further
2 minutes, stirring gently.
Add the wine and allow the
mixture to boil for 2-3
minutes. Set aside to cool.
4. Beat together the eggs,
egg yolk, cream and tomato
purée. Stir in the shellfish
mixture with salt and pepper.
5. Pour the mixture into the
pastry case, sprinkle over the
cheese, and bake in a
preheated oven at the lower
temperature for 30-35
minutes or until puffy and
browned. Serve with
buttered leaf spinach.

Dried Fruit and Spice Compôte

SERVES 6

100 g (4 oz) dried figs
100 g (4 oz) dried apricots
50 g (2 oz) dried apple
100 g (4 oz) dried prunes
50 g (2 oz) raisins
50 g (2 oz) sultanas
50 g (2 oz) currants
1 teaspoon mixed spice
3 tablespoons cooking brandy
150 ml (¼ pint) strong black
  coffee
150 ml (¼ pint) water

PREPARATION TIME: *10 minutes,*
  plus cooling

COOKING TIME: *15 minutes*

This dish is full of
nourishment and may be
served with a little cream for
a lunch or supper dessert, or
with bran and milk for a
delicious breakfast dish.

1. Place all the ingredients in
a large saucepan and bring
gently to the boil. Simmer for
5-6 minutes.
2. Turn the contents of the
pan into a large mixing bowl,
cover with a clean tea towel,
and allow to go quite cold.
3. Turn the compôte into a
large glass or earthenware
pot, seal, and allow to stand in
a cool place for at least 12
hours before using.

NOTE:
The compôte may be heated
if you wish, but never return
any hot leftovers to the main
compôte, as all will go bad. If
it is properly stored in a cold
place, you may add more
fruit, cold liquid and brandy
(which acts as a preservative).
If well sealed, it will keep for
more than 2 weeks.

Evening Meal
NOVEMBER

BAKED EGGS WITH MUSHROOMS

BUTTERED TOAST

CASSEROLE OF RABBIT
IN RED WINE

BRUSSELS SPROUTS

CREAMED POTATOES

ALMOND AND FIG BAKED APPLES

Baked Eggs with Mushrooms

SERVES 6

butter, for greasing
100 g (4 oz) small fresh button
 mushrooms, sliced
6 rashers streaky bacon, grilled
 and crumbled
6 eggs
6 tablespoons single cream
6 thin slices butter
salt
freshly ground black pepper
fingers of buttered toast, to
 serve

PREPARATION TIME: *10 minutes*

COOKING TIME: *10-20 minutes*

OVEN: *160°C, 325°F, Gas Mark 3*

1. Grease 6 individual ramekin dishes or small pots with butter.
2. Divide the mushrooms and bacon between the dishes, then break an egg into each dish.
3. Top each one with a tablespoon of cream, a thin slice of butter and salt and pepper.
4. Place the dishes on a baking sheet and cook in a preheated oven until the eggs are done to your liking.
5. Serve with fingers of buttered toast.

Casserole of Rabbit in Red Wine

SERVES 6

50 g (2 oz) butter
2 tablespoons oil
1 Spanish onion, peeled and chopped
3 medium carrots, peeled and diced
75 g (3 oz) streaky bacon, rinded and chopped
1 clove garlic, crushed
1 x 1·25 kg (2½ lb) rabbit, jointed
seasoned flour
300 ml (½ pint) red wine
300 ml (½ pint) stock
bouquet garni
12 prunes
salt
freshly ground black pepper

TO SERVE:
sprigs of parsley
croûtons of bread, fried in oil and drained

PREPARATION TIME: *20 minutes*
COOKING TIME: *2-2½ hours*
OVEN: *160°C, 325°F, Gas Mark 3*

1. Melt the butter and oil in a large saucepan and add the vegetables, bacon and garlic. Fry gently, stirring, until pale brown. Transfer the vegetables and bacon to a large ovenproof casserole, using a slotted spoon.
2. Dip the rabbit joints in seasoned flour, and fry them in the saucepan until lightly browned, then add them to the casserole.
3. Pour in the wine and stock, add the bouquet garni and prunes and cover.
4. Cook in a preheated moderate oven for 1½-2 hours, or until the rabbit is tender.
5. Remove the rabbit joints to a serving dish and keep warm. Check the sauce for seasoning, remove the bouquet garni and pour the sauce over the rabbit.
6. Garnish with parsley sprigs and piles of croûtons at either end of the dish. Serve with Brussels sprouts and creamed potatoes.

Almond and Fig Baked Apples

SERVES 6

6 Bramley cooking apples
50 g (2 oz) butter
400 g (14 oz) dried figs, chopped
6 tablespoons ground almonds
3 tablespoons sherry
cream or custard, to serve

PREPARATION TIME: *15 minutes*
COOKING TIME: *35 minutes*
OVEN: *180°C, 350°F, Gas Mark 4*

This easily prepared dessert relies on the delicious flavour of Bramley cooking apples. It is also simple to invent your own fillings from ingredients that you have in your store-cupboard.

1. Wash and dry the apples and remove the cores. Make a circular cut around the waist of each apple. Place in a roasting tin.
2. Melt half the butter in a small saucepan and add the figs, the almonds and the sherry. Stir over a high heat for 5 minutes.
3. Fill the apples with this mixture and top each one with a little of the remaining butter.
4. Cook in a preheated oven for 25-30 minutes, depending on the size of the apple.
5. Serve with cream or custard.

VARIATION:
There are endless different stuffings for baked apples. Keep your fillings tasty but reasonably dry, then use honey, golden syrup, treacle or maple syrup to pour over the apples during the cooking. Baste the apples with the juices during the cooking period.

Robert Carrier's Dinner Party

NOVEMBER

TOMATO AND
MOZZARELLA SALAD

GREEN PASTA

VEAL SCALLOPINI MIRABEAU

BUTTERED POTATOES

COFFEE RUM ICE CREAM GÂTEAU

The Tomato and mozzarella salad is an Italian-inspired, fresh-tasting salad that I often serve as an *antipasto*, to be followed by a second course of *pasta*, as in this menu.

The main course presents a new way with thinly sliced breaded cutlets of veal. Serve the Veal scallopini Mirabeau with green bean bundles (haricots verts, crisp-cooked and tied with strips of red pimento) and for those for whom no meal is complete without potatoes, I include a recipe for deep-fried potato balls, 'finished off' at the last minute in a little butter and olive oil.

The frozen coffee-chocolate-meringue extravaganza, prepared ahead of time, makes a delightful ending to the meal.

Coffee rum ice cream gâteau
(recipe page 109)

Tomato and Mozzarella Salad

SERVES 4

6 ripe tomatoes, thinly sliced
225 g (8 oz) mozzarella cheese,
  thinly sliced
6 tablespoons olive oil
2 tablespoons lemon juice
2 tablespoons chopped fresh
  basil or chives
salt
freshly ground black pepper
4 olives, halved and stoned, to
  garnish

PREPARATION TIME: *about*
  10 minutes

A deliciously simple Italian salad prepared in a matter of moments.

1. Arrange the tomato and mozzarella cheese slices in an alternating pattern on 4 individual serving plates.
2. Blend together the olive oil, lemon juice and chopped basil or chives and season with salt and pepper to taste. Pour the dressing over the tomatoes and cheese and garnish with olive halves.

Green Pasta

SERVES 4

salt
225 g (8 oz) medium-sized
  pasta shells
150 g (5 oz) frozen broccoli,
  thawed
100 g (4 oz) frozen peas
100 g (4 oz) courgettes
25 g (1 oz) butter
2 tablespoons chicken stock
freshly ground black pepper
8-12 cooked asparagus spears,
  cut into 4 cm (1½ inch)
  segments
50 ml (2 fl oz) double cream
2 tablespoons fresh Parmesan
  cheese, grated

PREPARATION TIME: *10 minutes*
COOKING TIME: *30-40 minutes*

Continuing the Italian flavour of this dinner party, the pasta dish makes a light extra course to serve between the salad and the veal.

1. Bring a large saucepan of salted water to the boil. Add the pasta shells, stirring with a fork to prevent shells from sticking together, and cook for 15 to 20 minutes, or until tender, but still *al dente:* a piece should be cooked but still firm when tested. As soon as the pasta shells are cooked, drain and set aside, whilst cooking the vegetables.
2. Trim the stalks from the broccoli and cook in boiling salted water for 3 minutes. Add the peas and cook for a further 3 minutes. Drain and refresh under cold running water, then drain again and set aside.
3. Cut each courgette lengthways into 8 pieces. Slice each piece into 4 cm (1½ inch) segments. Blanch the segments in boiling salted water for 2 to 3 minutes. Drain and refresh under cold running water, then drain again.
4. Transfer the courgettes to a shallow saucepan. Add the butter and chicken stock and season with pepper to taste. Cover and simmer for 5 minutes, or until the liquid has almost disappeared and the courgettes are tender.
5. Add the broccoli, peas and asparagus spears to the pan and toss over a high heat for 1 to 2 minutes to combine the flavours.
6. Add the pasta shells and double cream to the pan, toss well and heat through. Taste and adjust the seasoning. Transfer to a heated serving dish; sprinkle with grated Parmesan cheese and serve immediately.

Veal Scallopini Mirabeau

SERVES 4

2 veal cutlets, about 275 g
  (10 oz) each, boned, or 4 thin
  slices veal fillet
25 g (1 oz) flour
1 egg, beaten
75 g (3 oz) fine dry white
  breadcrumbs, sieved
4-6 tablespoons butter
2 tablespoons olive oil
salt
freshly ground black pepper
anchovy fillets, cut in half
  lengthways
stuffed olives, sliced
1 lemon, cut into wedges, to
  garnish

PREPARATION TIME: *20 minutes,*
  plus chilling
COOKING TIME: *about 10*
  minutes

This is one of my favourite ways of preparing veal. Boned cutlets are a good alternative to thin slices of veal cut across the grain from the leg. Make sure your veal slice is thin, but not transparent. You do not want to end up with a fried breadcrumb sandwich.

1. If boned cutlets are used, cut each one into 2 thin slices horizontally, so that you cut as much across the grain as possible. Lay the veal pieces between 2 sheets of greaseproof paper and, using a meat mallet or a rolling pin, pound until thin. Sprinkle with a little of the flour.
2. Pour the beaten egg into a shallow dish. Place the breadcrumbs in another shallow dish. Dip the veal pieces in the beaten egg, draining carefully, then roll in the breadcrumbs, patting the coating on firmly. Chill for at least 30 minutes to set.
3. Use 1 large frying pan, or 2 smaller ones, which will hold all the veal pieces comfortably in a single layer. Melt the butter with olive oil.

When the butter is foaming, sprinkle lightly with salt and pepper. Add the veal pieces and fry over a moderate heat for 3 to 5 minutes on one side. Turn them and arrange a lattice of anchovy strips on each piece of veal. Place a slice of stuffed olive in the centre of each 'lattice' opening and continue cooking for a further 3 to 5 minutes, or until the breadcrumbs are crisp and golden and the veal is cooked, but still juicy.
4. Transfer to a heated serving dish. Garnish with lemon wedges and serve.

Buttered Potatoes

SERVES 4

1 kg (2 lb) potatoes, peeled
oil, for deep frying
salt
freshly ground black pepper
2 tablespoons butter
1 tablespoon olive oil
2 tablespoons fresh parsley,
finely chopped, to garnish

PREPARATION TIME: *15 minutes,*
plus soaking

COOKING TIME: *about 25*
minutes

1. Cut the potatoes into small balls with a melon baller. Soak in iced water for 1 hour. Drain on paper towels.
2. Heat the oil in a large frying pan, or deep-fat fryer, to 190°C, 375°F: or when a cube of bread will brown in 60 seconds. Fry the balls in batches until golden, about 5 minutes per batch. Remove from the pan with a slotted spoon and drain on paper towels. Season generously.
3. Just before serving, shallow-fry the potato balls in the butter and olive oil for about 5 minutes, or until brown and cooked through. Drain on paper towels.
4. Place in a heated serving dish, sprinkle with parsley and serve immediately.

Coffee Rum Ice Cream Gâteau

SERVES 6-8

oil, for greasing
225 g (8 oz) caster sugar
3 egg whites (size 1, 2), whisked
until stiff
450 ml (¾ pint) double cream
1 tablespoon instant coffee
2 tablespoons boiling water
2 tablespoons dark Jamaican
rum
150 ml (5 fl oz) chocolate ice
cream

PREPARATION TIME: *about 30*
minutes, plus cooling and
freezing

COOKING TIME: *1 hour*

OVEN: *150°C, 300°F, Gas Mark 2*

1. Lightly oil 2 baking sheets.
2. Whisk 50 g (2 oz) of the caster sugar into the egg whites and continue whisking for 1 minute, or until stiff. Using a metal spoon, fold in the remaining sugar.
3. Place the meringue mixture in a piping bag and pipe small rosettes on to the prepared baking sheets, spacing them well apart. Bake in a preheated oven for 1 hour. Turn off the heat and leave in the oven for a further 10 to 15 minutes, or until they are crisp on the outside, but still soft in the centre. Allow to cool.
4. In a large bowl, whisk the cream until it forms soft peaks. In a small bowl, dilute the coffee with the boiling water. Allow to cool.
5. Reserve 4 attractive meringues for decoration, then fold the rest into the cream together with the coffee and rum, trying not to break the meringues.
6. Line the base of an 18 cm (7 inch) round loose-bottomed cake tin and spoon in the cream mixture; cover and freeze. Place the ice cream in the refrigerator to soften.
7. When the gâteau is hard, remove it from the freezer. Run a sharp knife around the edge and turn it out on to a flat plate. Carefully remove the base of the tin and peel off the greaseproof paper.
8. Beat the ice cream to soften it a little, then spoon it into a piping bag, fitted with a 1 cm (½ inch) star nozzle. Pipe rosettes around the top to decorate. Return to the freezer to harden.
9. Before serving, transfer the gâteau to a serving dish; decorate with the reserved meringues and place in the refrigerator for 10 minutes to soften slightly.
(Pictured on page 107.)

Tomato and mozzarella salad; Green pasta; Buttered potatoes; Veal scallopini Mirabeau

AUTUMN VEGETABLE SOUP
SPICED SAUSAGE MEAT PLAIT
CURRIED SPARE RIBS OF PORK
HERB CRUNCH LAMB CUTLETS
FISH PASTIES
FIRE-BAKED POTATOES WITH
SAVOURY BUTTERS
TOFFEE APPLES
CITRUS TODDY
SPICED WINE PUNCH

Curried Spare Ribs of Pork

SERVES 12

12 large spare ribs
150 ml (¼ pint) runny honey
1 teaspoon Worcester sauce
2 teaspoons mild curry paste
40 g (1½ oz) butter
2 teaspoons tomato purée
salt
freshly ground black pepper
25 g (1 oz) blanched almonds

PREPARATION TIME: *20 minutes*
COOKING TIME: *45 minutes*
OVEN: *190°C, 375°F, Gas Mark 5*

1. Arrange the spare ribs in a buttered roasting tin.
2. In a small saucepan melt together the honey, Worcester sauce, curry paste, butter, tomato purée, salt and pepper. Stir over a gentle heat until all is well incorporated. Finely chop the almonds, then add to the pan.
3. Pour this mixture over the spare ribs, place in a preheated oven and cook for 45 minutes, basting every 10 minutes.

Herb Crunch Lamb Cutlets

SERVES 12

12 lamb cutlets from the best end of neck
225 g (8 oz) brown breadcrumbs
1 tablespoon dried mint
1 tablespoon thyme
2 tablespoons grated Parmesan cheese
salt
freshly ground black pepper
2 eggs, beaten

PREPARATION TIME: *30 minutes*
COOKING TIME: *30 minutes*
OVEN: *200°C, 400°F, Gas Mark 6*

1. Trim the excess fat from the cutlets, and scrape the bones to form a handle. The excess trimmings may be rendered down for dripping.
2. Mix together the breadcrumbs, mint, thyme, cheese, salt and pepper.
3. Grease 2 baking sheets. Dip the cutlets first into the beaten egg, and then coat well with the breadcrumb mixture and lay them on the greased trays.
4. Bake in a preheated oven for 30 minutes.
5. Serve hot or cold.

Autumn Vegetable Soup

SERVES 12

50 g (2 oz) butter
350 g (12 oz) chuck steak, finely diced
450 g (1 lb) potatoes, peeled and finely diced
3 onions, peeled and finely chopped
4 leeks, cut into thin rings
450 g (1 lb) carrots, peeled and cut into thin strips
1 small cabbage, finely shredded
1 small cauliflower, cut into small florets
2 beef stock cubes
2.25 litres (4 pints) water
salt
freshly ground black pepper

PREPARATION TIME: *40 minutes*
COOKING TIME: *1½ hours*

1. Melt the butter in a large saucepan, add the meat, toss gently in the hot butter and remove from the pan.
2. Place all the prepared vegetables into the pan juices and stir over a gentle heat to coat with the butter.
3. Return the meat to the pot. Dissolve the stock cubes in the water and pour over the meat and vegetables. Add salt and pepper and simmer gently over a low heat for 1½ hours.
4. Remove the soup from the heat if not wanted immediately. To serve, bring to the boil and check the seasoning. The soup may be liquidized, then reheated for a smoother texture.

Spiced Sausage Meat Plait

SERVES 12

1 x 450 g (1 lb) packet frozen puff pastry, thawed
450 g (1 lb) sausage meat
75 g (3 oz) Cheddar cheese, grated
1 tablespoon tomato purée
1 medium onion, peeled and finely chopped
pinch of paprika
salt
freshly ground black pepper
beaten egg, to glaze

PREPARATION TIME: *25 minutes*
COOKING TIME: *1 hour*
OVEN: *200°C, 400°F, Gas Mark 6; 160°C, 325°F, Gas Mark 3*

This dish is attractive to display in its entirety, and slices may be carved as required. It is important to use a good quality sausage meat, otherwise the plait may be a little greasy.

1. Roll out the pastry to a rectangle measuring 40 x 33 cm (16 x 12 inches). Gently mark 3 lengthways strips. Leaving the centre strip whole, slash the outer strips diagonally at 2.5 cm (1 inch) intervals.
2. Mix together the sausage meat, cheese, tomato purée, onion, paprika, salt and pepper.
3. Form this mixture into a thick sausage shape, and lay it down the centre of the pastry.
4. Fold in the top and bottom ends of the pastry, then plait the diagonal strips neatly over the filling.
5. Place the plait on a baking sheet, making sure that the ends are securely turned under. Brush the plait with beaten egg and place in a preheated oven for 20 minutes. Lower the heat and continue cooking the plait for a further 40 minutes. It can be served hot or cold.

Herb crunch lamb cutlets; Autumn vegetable soup; Curried spare ribs of pork; Spiced sausage meat plait

Fish Pasties

SERVES 12

450 g (1 lb) shortcrust pastry
beaten egg, to glaze

FILLING:
350 g (12 oz) fresh haddock
    fillets, skinned
200 ml (⅓ pint) milk
1 small onion, sliced
1 small carrot, peeled and
    roughly chopped
1 bay leaf
salt
freshly ground black pepper

SAUCE:
50 g (2 oz) butter
50 g (2 oz) flour
300 ml (½ pint) fish liquor
225 g (8 oz) peeled prawns
1 tablespoon chopped fresh
    parsley
salt
freshly ground black pepper

PREPARATION TIME: 20 minutes
COOKING TIME: 50 minutes
OVEN: 190°C, 375°F, Gas Mark 5

1. Place the haddock in a pan with the milk, onion, carrot, bay leaf, salt and pepper. Bring gently to the boil and simmer for 10 minutes.
2. Remove the pan from the heat and strain the contents, setting aside 300 ml (½ pint) of the cooking liquor for the sauce. Flake the haddock, discarding the onion, carrot and bay leaf.
3. To make the sauce, melt the butter in a saucepan, then stir in the flour. Cook the roux for 2-3 minutes, stirring all the time. Remove from the heat and slowly stir in the reserved liquor. Return the sauce to the heat and cook, stirring, until thick. Simmer gently for 4-5 minutes.
4. Remove the pan from the heat and stir in the flaked fish, prawns and parsley. Adjust the seasoning.
5. Roll out the pastry and cut into twelve 10 cm (4 inch) squares. Divide the filling between the squares and brush the edges with beaten egg. Fold the pastry over diagonally and crimp the edges.
6. Brush each pasty with beaten egg and place on lightly greased baking trays. Bake for 20 minutes in a preheated oven until golden brown. Allow to cool on a wire tray.
7. The pasties can be gently reheated for serving.

Fish pasties; Fire-baked potatoes with mustard and tabasco butters;

Fire-Baked Potatoes

SERVES 12

12 large potatoes
sea salt

PREPARATION TIME: 30 minutes
COOKING TIME: 1½ hours
OVEN: 220°C, 425°F, Gas Mark 7

It is important that the potatoes are cooked right through. For the fillings, try experimenting with different butters, such as garlic, herb, chive or ketchup butter.

Alternatively, split open the cooked potatoes and add some grated cheese or chopped onion.

1. Scrub the potatoes and make a zig-zag split down one side. While they are still wet dip each cut side in sea salt. Wrap each potato in foil, making sure that the join is over the cut side.
2. Cook the potatoes in a preheated oven for half an hour, then place them in the hot coals at the base of the fire to finish cooking for about 1 hour.
3. When completely cooked, open the foil and gently squeeze the potato until it opens up. Serve with either of the following butters.

Mustard Butter

4 teaspoons English mustard
2 teaspoons chopped parsley
225 g (8 oz) butter, creamed

1. Beat the mustard and parsley into the creamed butter until well incorporated.
2. Turn the mixture on to a small sheet of greaseproof paper and form into a sausage shape 2.5 cm (1 inch) in diameter.
3. Roll up in the greaseproof paper, and fold in the ends, preserving the sausage shape.
4. Chill until set, then unwrap and serve with the Fire-baked potatoes.

Tabasco Butter

2 teaspoons Tabasco
2 teaspoons tomato purée
dash of cayenne pepper
225 g (8 oz) butter, creamed

1. Beat the tabasco, tomato purée and pepper into the creamed butter.
2. Follow the recipe for Mustard butter (left).

Spiced Wine Punch

SERVES 12

2 bottles red wine
1 bottle white wine
2 oranges, thinly sliced
2 lemons, thinly sliced
16 cloves
1 teaspoon grated nutmeg
2 teaspoons ground cinnamon
225 g (8 oz) demerara sugar
fresh orange and lemon slices,
    to garnish

PREPARATION TIME: *20 minutes*

COOKING TIME: *1 hour*

This punch is best made at least 1 hour before drinking, and should be served hot.

1. Pour the wines into a large pan, and place over a very gentle heat.
2. Cut each orange and lemon slice into quarters and add to the pan. Stir in the remaining ingredients.
3. Warm the punch very gently, stirring occasionally until the sugar has dissolved.
4. Ladle the punch into individual glasses and garnish each one with a fresh orange or lemon slice.

Toffee apples; Spiced wine punch; Citrus toddy

Toffee Apples

SERVES 12

12 eating apples, washed, dried
    and stalks removed
12 wooden sticks
350 g (12 oz) sugar
12 drops cochineal
50 g (2 oz) butter
100 g (4 oz) golden syrup
1 teaspoon lemon juice
150 ml (¼ pint) water

PREPARATION TIME: *30 minutes*

COOKING TIME: *20 minutes*

1. Push a wooden stick into each apple.
2. Place the sugar, cochineal, butter, golden syrup, lemon juice and water in a heavy-based pan. Stir gently over a low heat until the sugar has dissolved, then increase the heat and boil rapidly until the toffee registers 145°C (290°F) on the sugar thermometer, or, if the syrup is dropped into cold water, it will form brittle threads which snap easily.
3. Dip the apples into the pan one at a time, twisting the pan to coat evenly.
4. Immediately plunge each apple into a bowl of cold water to set the toffee, then stand on a piece of oiled greaseproof paper until cold.

Citrus Toddy

MAKES APPROXIMATELY 20 DRINKS

3 grapefruit
3 oranges
3 lemons
450 g (1 lb) sugar
1.2 litres (2 pints) water
25 g (1 oz) citric acid

PREPARATION TIME: *40 minutes,*
    plus overnight soaking

COOKING TIME: *25 minutes*

This fruit squash is strong in flavour. It can be watered down at a ratio of 1 part to 4 parts for children, or can be mixed with whisky, gin or vodka for cocktails.

1. Pare the rind from the fruits and place in a heavy-based pan.
2. Remove the pith and pips from the fruit and discard. Roughly chop the flesh and add it to the pan together with the sugar, water and citric acid.
3. Heat gently, stirring, until the sugar has dissolved, then raise the heat and simmer for 5 minutes.
4. Remove from the heat and allow to stand in a cool place overnight.
5. Strain off the citrus juice, discarding the pulp, and use as required.

Winter

Winter is the time when we want nourishing, comforting food and this is where English cooking comes into its own. A thick soup or broth makes a warm and welcoming start to a meal or a traditional English pudding will provide a nourishing and substantial finish.

VEGETABLES

In December, after November frosts, most vegetables are in perfect condition. Parsnips, Brussels sprouts and celery, in particular, are better after a frost. Some people disregard the English celery at this time in favour of the imported variety, because the English celery is often sold with a lot of earth on it, but its flavour is, in fact, much better.

Although there are still imported vegetables in the shops, make the most of the home-produced root vegetables, such as parsnips, swedes and turnips. These are essential to winter soups, stews and casseroles.

There are plenty of green vegetables about – Brussels sprouts and the green tops, leeks, kale and varieties of cabbage, such as Savoy and January King. White cabbage is delicious lightly braised with some onion and bacon. Red cabbage, as well as for pickling – the ideal accompaniment for hot-pots – is delicious when cooked with apples and goes well with pork and duck dishes.

Look out for the more unusual winter vegetables. Celeriac is a large root vegetable with a distinct celery flavour; peel it, cut it into cubes, cook it in salted water until tender, then serve it in a white sauce with some mustard powder in it if liked. Jersualem artichokes are like small knobbly potatoes, they have a very smoky flavour and make a delicious soup. They are best cooked in their jackets, then peeled when tender. As a vegetable, they should be served with melted butter or a white sauce. Salsify is a very thin root vegetable; peel and cook in lightly salted water to which a little lemon juice has been added to keep it white. Seakale is like thin celery. It is cooked in bundles in lightly salted water and is nicest when served with a Hollandaise sauce. Seakale, like leeks, can also be served cold in a vinaigrette dressing as the starter to a meal.

Many raw winter vegetables make delicious salads. What could be simpler than shredded white cabbage and grated carrot mixed together with mayonnaise to make coleslaw? Red cabbage, celery and apples make a wonderful accompaniment to cold meat. Experiment with shredded Brussels sprouts, small sliced leeks and grated root vegetables made up to your own combination, or try adding dried fruits and nuts to make even more unusual salads. These salads are best with a mayonnaise or yogurt-based dressing.

FRUIT

In December the shops are full of citrus fruits: Jaffa oranges from Israel, satsumas from Spain and the lovely seedless clementines which come mostly from North Africa. In January the Seville oranges for marmalade come in from Spain. These oranges freeze very well; just scrub the skins and dry thoroughly, then pack into polythene bags.

Bramley apples for cooking are plentiful, as are many varieties of English apples, such as Spartans, Cox's Orange Pippins, Laxton Superb and Golden Delicious. Look out for the delicious large red McIntosh apples, which are imported at this time of year from America and Canada. Also imported from America are cranberries, which have a short season around Christmas.

Around Christmastime the shops have the dried fruits, mostly imported from North Africa. Dates, figs and muscatels are delicious served at the end of a meal with some nuts, instead of a traditional pudding.

NUTS

Nuts are plentiful in winter: chestnuts to roast on the fire, to make the traditional chestnut stuffing for the Christmas turkey or to serve with the Brussels sprouts. But other nuts, especially Brazil nuts and walnuts, make a very good addition to stuffings.

GAME

There is plenty of poultry and game available in winter and game makes a very special dinner party in December, but after that until the end of the game season in February the birds tend to become tougher and therefore more suitable for casseroling.

MEAT

In winter, too, we tend to buy the cheaper cuts of meat for long slow cooking: neck of lamb, shin of beef and oxtail are perfect for making flavoursome casseroles and if you have a little red wine available, even a small glassful will enhance the flavour of a casserole and make it into something special.

FISH

Although available all the year round, the oily types of fish are very suitable for winter meals, especially as this is when we tend to have the more substantial breakfasts and the often neglected high tea. Kippers and herrings, especially when cooked in oatmeal, make delicious breakfasts and teas. Other smoked fish, such as mackerel, can be made into a variety of dishes – pâtés, quiches and hot-pots.

TABLE ARRANGEMENTS

Especially around Christmas it is nice to decorate the table, but fresh flowers in winter are often scarce and expensive, so make the most of the wonderful greenery that abounds; mixed with some dried flowers, with perhaps a red candle and some red ribbon, it will make a lovely seasonal centrepiece for your table.

Lunch or Supper

(DECEMBER)

MACARONI WITH AUBERGINE,
MOZZARELLA AND TOMATO

BAKED APPLES

Macaroni with Aubergine, Mozzarella and Tomato

SERVES 4

350 g (12 oz) aubergines, thinly sliced
salt
225 g (8 oz) macaroni
25 g (1 oz) plain flour
3-4 tablespoons oil
175 g (6 oz) Mozzarella cheese, sliced
225 g (8 oz) tomatoes, skinned and sliced
1 teaspoon dried basil
freshly ground black pepper
1 tablespoon Parmesan cheese

PREPARATION TIME: *30 minutes*

COOKING TIME: *45 minutes*

OVEN: *180°C, 350°F, Gas Mark 4*

1. Put the aubergine slices into a colander. Sprinkle with salt, cover with a plate and leave for 30 minutes.
2. Cook the macaroni in a large pan of lightly salted water for 10-12 minutes. Drain well.
3. Rinse the aubergine slices and dry well. Coat in flour and fry in the oil until lightly browned on each side. Drain on paper towels.
4. In a greased ovenproof casserole put one-third of the macaroni, one-third of the Mozzarella, half the aubergine slices, half the tomatoes and half the basil. Sprinkle with salt and pepper. Repeat the layers once more, then put a final layer of macaroni and Mozzarella.
5. Sprinkle the Parmesan cheese over the top. Place in a preheated oven for 30 minutes.
6. The baked apples can be placed in the oven at the same time. Once the macaroni has been taken out, increase the temperature to 200°C, 400°F, Gas Mark 6 and continue cooking while you eat the macaroni.

Evening Meal
DECEMBER

BURGUNDY MUSHROOMS

PORK AND LIVER HOT-POT

PICKLED RED CABBAGE

CRANBERRY UPSIDE-DOWN CAKE

Burgundy Mushrooms

SERVES 4

3 tablespoons olive oil
1 onion, peeled and chopped
1 garlic clove, crushed
350 g (12 oz) button
  mushrooms
100 g (4 oz) cooked smoked
  ham, cut into strips
1 teaspoon mixed herbs
150 ml (¼ pint) red wine
salt
freshly ground black pepper
hot French bread, to serve

PREPARATION TIME: *10 minutes,*
  plus marinating

COOKING TIME: *20 minutes*

OVEN: *220°C, 425°F, Gas Mark 7*

The wine is an important part of this dish and it is a good opportunity to use up any leftovers from a bottle of red wine.

1. Melt the oil in a pan, add the onion and garlic and cook until soft.
2. Add the mushrooms, ham, herbs, red wine, salt and pepper to the pan. Bring to the boil, then turn off the heat and leave to marinate for about 30 minutes.
3. Divide the mixture between 4 large ramekin dishes. Place in a preheated oven for 15 minutes. Serve with hot French bread.

Pork and Liver Hot-Pot

SERVES 4

2 large spare rib pork chops,
  boned
225 g (8 oz) pig's liver, in one
  piece
15 g (½ oz) lard
1 onion, peeled and sliced
2 carrots, peeled and sliced
1 turnip, peeled and diced
1 small cooking apple, peeled
  and diced
150 ml (¼ pint) stock
1 teaspoon dried sage
salt
freshly ground black pepper
450 g (1 lb) potatoes, peeled
  and sliced

PREPARATION TIME: *15 minutes*

COOKING TIME: *about 2½ hours*

OVEN: *160°C, 325°F, Gas Mark 3;*
  220°C, 425°F, Gas Mark 7

1. Cut the pork and liver into cubes.
2. Melt the lard in a pan, add the pork and liver and cook until brown on all sides.
3. Transfer to an ovenproof casserole, then add the vegetables, apple, stock, dried sage, salt and pepper. Mix well.
4. Top the casserole with the sliced potatoes. Cover with a lid or foil. Place in a preheated oven for about 2 hours.
5. Remove the lid or foil, increase the heat and cook for a further 30 minutes to brown the potato topping.
6. Serve hot with pickled red cabbage.

VARIATION:
The liver in this recipe can be substituted with an equal quantity of pig's kidney.

Cranberry Upside-Down Cake

SERVES 4

175 g (6 oz) cranberries
150 ml (¼ pint) water
100 g (4 oz) butter
100 g (4 oz) caster sugar
1 egg, beaten
100 g (4 oz) self-raising flour,
   sifted
grated rind of 1 orange
1 tablespoon orange juice
1 tablespoon redcurrant jelly

PREPARATION TIME: *20 minutes*

COOKING TIME: *45 minutes*

OVEN: *180°C, 350°F, Gas Mark 4*

1. Put the cranberries into a pan with the water, bring to the boil, then simmer gently for a few minutes until they pop.
2. Grease and line an 18 cm (7 inch) sandwich tin. Melt together 25 g (1 oz) of the butter and 25 g (1 oz) of the caster sugar and put into the sandwich tin. Add the strained cranberries.
3. Cream together the remaining 75 g (3 oz) butter and 75 g (3 oz) caster sugar until light and fluffy. Beat in the egg, then lightly fold in the flour, orange rind and juice. Spread the mixture over the top of the cranberries.
4. Place in a preheated oven for 30 minutes. The cake is cooked when it springs back after being gently pressed with a finger. Turn out upside down and leave to cool on a wire tray.
5. Place the redcurrant jelly in a small pan over a gentle heat until melted. Brush over the cranberries to glaze.

NOTE:
Cranberries, imported from the U.S.A., have a very short season. They can be used in sweet dishes as here or in a sauce as an accompaniment for poultry and game dishes.

Dinner Party
DECEMBER

FEUILLETÉ AUX BLANCS DE POIREAUX

ROAST PARTRIDGE WITH PORT
AND REDCURRANT SAUCE

CELERIAC PURÉE

BRUSSELS SPROUTS

CLEMENTINES IN ORANGE LIQUEUR

ALMOND PETIT FOURS

Feuilleté aux Blancs de Poireaux

SERVES 4

1 x 375 g (13 oz) pack frozen
*   puff pastry, thawed*
1 egg, beaten
50 g (2 oz) butter
350 g (12 oz) white part of
*   leeks, thinly sliced*
juice of ½ lemon
salt
freshly ground black pepper
1 x 150 ml (5 fl oz) carton
*   double cream*
4 sprigs parsley, to garnish

PREPARATION TIME: *15 minutes*

COOKING TIME: *20 minutes*

OVEN: *220°C, 425°F, Gas Mark 7*

1. Roll out the pastry to a rectangle 26 cm x 15 cm (10 inches x 6 inches). Cut into 4 pieces, each 13 cm x 7½ cm (5 inches x 3 inches).

2. Score each piece lightly in a diamond pattern and brush the tops with beaten egg. Place on a wetted baking sheet and bake in a preheated oven for 20 minutes.

3. Meanwhile, prepare the filling. Melt the butter in a pan, add the leeks and cook gently for about 10 minutes until soft but not browned.

4. Add the lemon juice, salt and pepper to the leeks, stir well, then add the cream. Bring to the boil, stirring constantly. Cook for 2-3 minutes.

5. When the pastry slices are cooked, remove from the oven and cut each one in half horizontally. Divide the leek mixture between the bottom halves of the pastry slices, then replace the pastry top. Serve immediately, garnished with parsley sprigs.

Roast Partridge with Port and Redcurrant Sauce

SERVES 4

25 g (1 oz) butter
4 partridges
8 small rashers streaky bacon, rinded

SAUCE:

1 tablespoon cornflour
½ teaspoon ground ginger
85 ml (3 fl oz) port
150 ml (¼ pint) water
2 tablespoons redcurrant jelly
salt
freshly ground black pepper

TO GARNISH:

1 bunch watercress
potato crisps

PREPARATION TIME: *10 minutes*

COOKING TIME: *about 1 hour 5 minutes*

OVEN: *220°C, 425°F, Gas Mark 7*

1. Spread the butter over the partridges. Put the bacon over the breasts, then place them in a roasting pan. Put in a preheated oven for 50-60 minutes.
2. Remove the partridges from the oven. Transfer to a serving dish and keep warm while you make the sauce.
3. Pour off most of the fat from the roasting pan, leaving about 1 tablespoonful. Place the pan over the heat. Stir in the cornflour and ground ginger. Cook for 2-3 minutes.
4. Add the port, water, redcurrant jelly, salt and pepper. Bring to the boil then cook for 2-3 minutes. Strain into a sauceboat.
5. Garnish the partridges with watercress and potato crisps. Serve with Celeriac purée (see right) and Brussels sprouts.

NOTE:
Partridges are small game birds, and usually only serve one person each. However, if they are particularly large, then half each will be sufficient.

Celeriac Purée

SERVES 4

1 celeriac, about 450 g (1 lb), peeled and diced
salt
150 ml (¼ pint) single cream
25 g (1 oz) butter
pinch English mustard powder
freshly ground black pepper

PREPARATION TIME: *15 minutes*

COOKING TIME: *15-20 minutes*

1. Put the celeriac into a pan of lightly salted water, bring to the boil, then simmer for 15-20 minutes until tender.
2. Strain the celeriac, put into a blender or food processor with the cream, butter, mustard powder and pepper, and blend to a thick purée.
3. Reheat gently if necessary.

Almond Petit Fours

MAKES ABOUT 24 BISCUITS

100 g (4 oz) ground almonds
100 g (4 oz) caster sugar
few drops almond essence
2 egg whites, whisked until stiff
flaked almonds or glacé
cherries, to decorate

PREPARATION TIME: *15 minutes*

COOKING TIME: *20-25 minutes*

OVEN: *150°C, 300°F, Gas Mark 2*

1. Stir the ground almonds, caster sugar and almond essence into the egg whites.
2. Line a baking sheet with non-stick silicone or greased greaseproof paper. Place the mixture into a piping bag with a large star nozzle and pipe the mixture into circles, S-shapes and sticks. Put a flaked almond or piece of glacé cherry on each one.
3. Place in a preheated oven for 20-25 minutes. Cool on a wire tray.

Clementines in Orange Liqueur

SERVES 4

175 g (6 oz) caster sugar
600 ml (1 pint) water
8 clementines, peeled and pith
removed
2 tablespoons orange liqueur

PREPARATION TIME: *10 minutes,*
plus cooling

COOKING TIME: *20-25 minutes*

1. Put the sugar and water into a large pan, bring to the boil, stirring constantly until the sugar has dissolved.
2. Add the clementines, bring to the boil, then simmer gently for about 10 minutes. Leave to cool in the liquid.
3. Remove the fruit, boil down the syrup until reduced to about 300 ml (½ pint). Cool, then add the liqueur. Pour over the clementines.

Winter Breakfast
JANUARY

HERBY PORK SAUSAGES

APPLE PANCAKES

BRAN AND RAISIN MUFFINS

SEVILLE ORANGE MARMALADE

The sausages can be made in advance, as can the batter for the apple pancakes. The Bran and raisin muffins can be made beforehand and reheated to serve.

Herby Pork Sausages

SERVES 4

750 g (1½ lb) lean belly of pork, trimmed, boned and skinned
25 g (1 oz) white breadcrumbs
1 tablespoon milk
¼ teaspoon ground mace
1 teaspoon ground sage
salt
freshly ground black pepper
seasoned flour
lard, for frying

PREPARATION TIME: *15 minutes*

COOKING TIME: *10-15 minutes*

1. Finely mince the pork twice or grind in a food processor. (You may be able to buy pork ready-minced in some supermarkets or your butcher may mince it for you.)
2. Put the minced pork in a bowl, add the breadcrumbs, milk, mace, dried sage, salt and pepper. Mix well.
3. Form into 8 sausage shapes. Roll in seasoned flour and fry gently until brown on all sides.

Apple Pancakes

MAKES 8 PANCAKES

175 g (6 oz) plain flour, sifted
1½ teaspoons bicarbonate of soda
25 g (1 oz) caster sugar
1 egg, beaten
250 ml (8 fl oz) milk
25 g (1 oz) butter, melted
1 large cooking apple, peeled and grated
lard, for frying
warmed maple syrup, to serve

PREPARATION TIME: *10 minutes*

COOKING TIME: *10-15 minutes*

1. Put the flour into a bowl with the bicarbonate of soda and sugar. Beat in the egg, milk and melted butter. Stir in the grated apple.
2. Melt a little of the lard in a large frying pan, make 4 pancakes by putting 2 tablespoons of the mixture for each pancake into the pan. Cook gently until the underside has browned and bubbles burst on the surface. Turn and cook until brown.
3. Repeat for the next 4. Serve with maple syrup.

Bran and Raisin Muffins

MAKES 12

50 g (2 oz) bran
250 ml (8 fl oz) milk
50 g (2 oz) caster sugar
50 g (2 oz) white cooking fat, whipped up
1 egg, beaten
100 g (4 oz) plain flour, sifted
½ teaspoon salt
3 teaspoons baking powder
100 g (4 oz) raisins
lard, for greasing

PREPARATION TIME: *20 minutes*

COOKING TIME: *25 minutes*

OVEN: *180°C, 350°F, Gas Mark 4*

1. Soak the bran in the milk for 10 minutes.
2. Cream together the sugar and fat until light and fluffy, stir in the egg, bran and milk.
3. Lightly fold in the flour, salt, baking powder and raisins. The mixture will remain a little lumpy.
4. Grease 12 muffin tins or deep patty tins well and divide the mixture between them. Place in a preheated oven for 25 minutes. Serve warm.

Seville Orange Marmalade

MAKES APPROX. 2.75 KG (6 LB)

1 kg (2 lb) Seville oranges
1 lemon
2.25 litres (4 pints) water
2 kg (4 lb) preserving sugar

PREPARATION TIME: *15 minutes*

COOKING TIME: *2-2½ hours*

Seville oranges have a very short season around January, however if you wish to make marmalade later in the year, they can be stored in the freezer quite successfully.

1. Cut the fruit in half and squeeze out the juice. Remove the pips and tie in a muslin bag.
2. Finely shred the fruit peel, put it into a large pan with the juice, water and muslin bag. Bring to the boil, then simmer for about 1½ hours, until the peel is soft and the liquid reduced to about half.
3. Remove the muslin bag, and squeeze out any liquid from it.
4. Add the sugar to the pan and stir well until completely dissolved. Bring to the boil and continue boiling until setting point is reached.
5. To test if the mixture has set, put a little of the marmalade on to a cold saucer. Leave until cold, then if it forms a 'skin' when pushed slightly, the setting point has been reached.
6. Put the marmalade into warmed jars, cover with waxed discs and seal well with cellophane covers.

CLOCKWISE FROM THE BOTTOM:
Apple pancakes;
Bran and raisin muffins;
Seville orange marmalade;
Herby pork sausages

Lunch or Supper
(JANUARY)

LAMB, BARLEY AND
VEGETABLE BROTH

SODA BREAD

STILTON CHEESE AND CELERY

Lamb, Barley and Vegetable Broth

SERVES 4

450 g (1 lb) middle neck of
   lamb
1.2 litres (2 pints) water
salt
freshly ground black pepper
1 large carrot, peeled and diced
1 large parsnip, peeled and
   diced
1 large onion, peeled and
   chopped
1 large leek, sliced
40 g (1½ oz) pearl barley
1 tablespoon chopped fresh
   parsley, to garnish

PREPARATION TIME: *15 minutes*

COOKING TIME: *2-2½ hours*

1. Put the lamb into a large pan with the water, salt and pepper. Bring to the boil, skimming off any scum that rises to the surface and simmer for 1 hour.
2. Remove the pan from the heat. Take out the meat, remove and discard the bones. Cut the meat into cubes then return it to the broth with the vegetables and barley.
3. Bring to the boil and simmer for a further 1-1½ hours. Sprinkle with chopped parsley, to garnish and serve with Soda bread (see below).

Soda Bread

MAKES 1 LOAF

225 g (8 oz) plain flour, sifted
225 g (8 oz) wholemeal flour
1 teaspoon bicarbonate of soda
2 teaspoons salt
25 g (1 oz) butter
300 ml (½ pint) buttermilk
water, if necessary
lard, for greasing

PREPARATION TIME: *10 minutes*

COOKING TIME: *35-40 minutes*

OVEN: *200°C, 400°F, Gas Mark 6*

1. In a large bowl mix together the flours, bicarbonate of soda and salt. Rub in the butter.
2. Pour in the buttermilk and mix to a soft dough, adding a little water if a little dry.
3. Knead the mixture lightly then form into a round shape. Put on to a greased baking sheet. Cut a deep cross in the top of the loaf.
4. Place in a preheated oven for 35-40 minutes. Cool on a wire tray.

Evening Meal
JANUARY

PARSNIP SOUP

OXTAIL WITH ORANGE AND WALNUTS

BRAISED WHITE CABBAGE

APPLE MERINGUE PIE

Parsnip Soup

SERVES 4

25 g (1 oz) butter
450 g (1 lb) parsnips, peeled
    and chopped
1 medium onion, peeled and
    chopped
1 teaspoon curry powder
900 ml (1½ pints) beef stock
300 ml (½ pint) milk
salt
freshly ground black pepper
chopped parsley, to garnish

PREPARATION TIME: *10 minutes*

COOKING TIME: *1¼ hours*

1. Melt the butter in a large pan, add the parsnips and onion and cook gently for about 10 minutes, stirring frequently.
2. Add the curry powder to the pan, cook for 2-3 minutes, then add the stock, milk, salt and pepper. Bring to the boil and simmer for 1 hour.
3. Blend or sieve the soup. Reheat, taste and adjust the seasoning and sprinkle with parsley to serve.

VARIATION:
For a special occasion, replace 150 ml (¼ pint) of the milk with 150 ml (¼ pint) single cream.

Oxtail with Orange and Walnuts

SERVES 4

25 g (1 oz) flour
salt
freshly ground black pepper
1 large oxtail, jointed
25 g (1 oz) dripping
2 onions, peeled and sliced
2 carrots, peeled and sliced
150 ml (¼ pint) beef stock
grated rind and juice of
    2 oranges
1 bay leaf
50 g (2 oz) walnuts, chopped

PREPARATION TIME: *15 minutes*

COOKING TIME: *about 4 hours*

OVEN: *150°C, 300°F, Gas Mark 2*

When buying oxtail, it is important to choose meat that is lean. If the meat is a little fatty, it should be well trimmed of excess fat. As the casserole needs long, slow cooking, you will need to prepare it well in advance of serving.

1. Season the flour with salt and pepper. Coat the oxtail in the seasoned flour. Melt the dripping in a pan, brown the pieces of oxtail all over, then transfer to an ovenproof casserole.
2. Brown the onions and carrots in the pan, then add to the casserole. Pour in the stock, then add the orange rind and juice, bay leaf, salt and pepper.
3. Cover the casserole with foil or a lid. Place in a preheated oven for 3½-4 hours.
4. Remove from the oven to a serving dish. Remove the bay leaf and sprinkle with the chopped walnuts. Increase the oven heat as required for the Apple meringue pie (see next recipe).
5. Serve the oxtail with braised white cabbage.

Apple Meringue Pie

SERVES 4-6

450 g (1 lb) cooking apples,
    peeled and sliced
50 g (2 oz) caster sugar
25 g (1 oz) butter
grated rind of 1 lemon
150 ml (¼ pint) water
1 x 20 cm (8 inch) shortcrust
    pastry case, baked blind
2 eggs, separated
75 g (3 oz) caster sugar

PREPARATION TIME: *45 minutes*

COOKING TIME: *20-25 minutes*

OVEN: *180°C, 350°F, Gas Mark 4*

1. Put the apples in a pan with the sugar, butter, lemon rind and water. Cook gently until the apples are soft, then increase the heat and cook to a dry purée, stirring frequently.
2. Cool the mixture slightly, then beat in the egg yolks. Put the mixture into the pastry case.
3. Whisk the egg whites until stiff, whisk in the caster sugar, then spread the meringue over the top of the apples.
4. Place in a preheated oven for 10-15 minutes. Serve hot or cold.

VARIATION:
In the summer this pie is particularly delicious made with gooseberries instead of apples. The fruit is prepared in the same way, although it may be necessary to sieve the fruit purée to remove any coarse skins and pips.

Dinner Party

JANUARY

SMOKED SALMON AND
TARAMA TIMBALES

STUFFED LOIN OF PORK

BEETROOT WITH SOUR CREAM
AND CUMIN

PEARS POACHED IN LEMON JUICE
AND WHITE WINE

IRISH LACE COOKIES

Smoked Salmon and Tarama Timbales

SERVES 4

oil, for greasing
175 g (6 oz) smoked salmon,
*   thinly sliced*
175 g (6 oz) taramasalata
175 g (6 oz) full fat soft cheese
dash of Tabasco sauce
juice of ½ lemon
shake of cayenne pepper
4 twists of lemon, to garnish

PREPARATION TIME: *15 minutes,*
*   plus chilling*

Taramasalata is a cod's roe pâté. It can be used on its own as a starter or dip. It is available in supermarkets and delicatessens.

1. Oil 4 ramekin dishes. Line the dishes with smoked salmon and chop any that remains.
2. Mix together the taramasalata, soft cheese, Tabasco sauce, lemon juice and cayenne pepper. Add any remaining salmon. Divide between the 4 dishes. Level the tops and chill well for 2-3 hours.
3. Carefully turn out of the dishes and garnish with twists of lemon.

Stuffed Loin of Pork

SERVES 4

1 loin of pork, boned, skinned rolled and tied, 1 kg (2¼ lb) boned weight
1 small cooking apple, peeled, cored and chopped
8 prunes, stoned and chopped
25 g (1 oz) butter
150 ml (¼ pint) dry cider
150 ml (¼ pint) stock
salt
freshly ground black pepper
2 tablespoons clear honey
1 tablespoon French mustard
1 tablespoon plain flour

PREPARATION TIME: *15 minutes*

COOKING TIME: *1½ hours*

OVEN: *180°C, 350°F, Gas Mark 4;*
200°C, 400°F, Gas Mark 6

1. Make a large hole through the 'eye' of the pork with a sharpening steel or similar object.
2. Mix together the apple and prunes and stuff the hole with the mixture.
3. Melt the butter in a large frying pan and brown the pork on all sides. Transfer to a roasting tin, fat side up, pour over the cider and stock, and sprinkle with salt and pepper. Cover the tin with foil and place in a preheated oven for 1 hour.
4. Remove the tin from the oven. Remove and discard the foil. Pour off and reserve most of the juices, leaving enough to cover the bottom of the tin. Mix together the honey and mustard and brush over the pork. Increase the oven heat, replace the meat and cook for a further 30 minutes.
5. Remove the meat from the oven and keep warm. Put the roasting pan over the heat, stir in the flour, cook for 2-3 minutes, then pour in the reserved juices. Stir well to incorporate all the bits from the bottom of the tin. Bring to the boil, cook for 2-3 minutes, then strain the sauce.
6. Remove the strings from the pork. Slice thickly and serve with the sauce, accompanied by Beetroot with sour cream and cumin (see below).

NOTE:
Most butchers when they are not too busy will bone, skin and roll meat to your requirements. You might find that, at the same time, the butcher would be willing to make the hole in the meat with his sharpening steel. Reserve the bones to make the stock.

Beetroot with Sour Cream and Cumin

SERVES 4

25 g (1 oz) butter
2 teaspoons ground cumin
1 x 150 ml (5 fl oz) carton soured cream
450 g (1 lb) cooked beetroot, peeled and diced
salt
freshly ground black pepper

PREPARATION TIME: *5 minutes*

COOKING TIME: *5 minutes*

Many people think of beetroot as just a cold salad vegetable, but it makes a very unusual and delicious hot vegetable.

1. Melt the butter in a pan, add the cumin. Stir well and cook for 1-2 minutes.
2. Add the soured cream, beetroot, salt and pepper. Cook until the beetroot is heated through.

Pears Poached in Lemon Juice and White Wine

SERVES 4

rind and juice of 2 lemons
150 ml (¼ pint) white wine
150 ml (¼ pint) water
75 g (3 oz) caster sugar
4 firm pears, cored and peeled
2 teaspoons arrowroot

PREPARATION TIME: *20 minutes, plus cooling*

COOKING TIME: *35 minutes*

When buying pears for this dish, choose pears of the same size and shape, as this makes the presentation of the dish so much better. It is easier if you core the pears before peeling them. Use an apple corer or a sharp, thin-bladed knife and remove the core from the bottom of the pear. Leave the stalk to decorate if wished.

1. Put the lemon rind and juice into a saucepan with the white wine, water and sugar. Bring to the boil, stirring frequently, until the sugar has dissolved.
2. Put the pears into the pan and poach for about 30 minutes until they are tender, turning carefully from time to time. Remove from the heat and leave the pears in the pan to cool in the juice.
3. When quite cold, stand the pears in a serving dish. Mix the arrowroot with a little of the juice, pour back into the pan, bring to the boil, then cook for 2-3 minutes. Leave to cool, then strain over the pears.
4. Serve the poached pears accompanied by Irish lace cookies (see right).

Irish Lace Cookies

MAKES 24

100 g (4 oz) butter
100 g (4 oz) soft brown sugar
25 g (1 oz) self-raising flour,
  sifted
2 tablespoons milk
100 g (4 oz) rolled oats
1 teaspoon vanilla essence

PREPARATION TIME: *10 minutes*

COOKING TIME: *10 minutes*

OVEN: *180°C, 350°F, Gas Mark 4*

1. Cream together the butter and sugar until light and fluffy. Stir in the flour, milk, rolled oats and vanilla essence.

2. Drop teaspoonfuls of the mixture on to well-greased baking sheets, leaving room for the cookies to spread. Place in a preheated oven for 10 minutes. Leave for a few minutes on the baking sheet, then cool on a wire tray.

VARIATION:
These biscuits are called lace cookies due to their appearance once cooked: they spread out and often go into holes. They are delicious on their own and also make a good accompaniment to mousse and ice cream.

The vanilla essence could be substituted with some grated orange or lemon rind.

Lunch or Supper

FEBRUARY

FRIKADELLER
HOT POTATO SALAD
RED CABBAGE SALAD
CHESTNUT MOUSSE

Frikadeller

SERVES 4

225 g (8 oz) minced veal
225 g (8 oz) minced pork
1 small onion, peeled and
   grated
25 g (1 oz) plain flour
salt
freshly ground black pepper
1 teaspoon dried dill weed
1 egg, beaten
300 ml (½ pint) milk
25 g (1 oz) butter
2 tablespoons oil
lemon slices, to garnish

PREPARATION TIME: *15 minutes*

COOKING TIME: *15-20 minutes*

1. Put the veal, pork, onion, flour, salt, pepper and dill in a bowl. Mix thoroughly.
2. Beat in the egg, then add the milk gradually, beating well until the mixture is fluffy.
3. Melt the butter and oil together in a large frying pan.
4. Shape the mixture into oblongs with the help of 2 tablespoons. Drop into the pan and cook gently for 15-20 minutes, turning frequently, until brown on all sides.
5. Garnish with lemon slices and serve with Hot potato salad and Red cabbage salad (see next page).

Red Cabbage Salad

SERVES 4

350 g (12 oz) red cabbage,
 shredded
1 large Cox's apple, chopped
2 sticks celery, chopped
50 g (2 oz) stoned raisins
50 g (2 oz) walnuts chopped

DRESSING:
3 tablespoons mayonnaise
1 tablespoon white wine
 vinegar
1 tablespoon oil
1 garlic clove, peeled and
 crushed
1 teaspoon clear honey
1 teaspoon whole grain
 mustard
salt
freshly ground black pepper

PREPARATION TIME: *15 minutes*

Red cabbage makes an ideal
winter salad when traditional
salad greens are expensive
and not at their best. It is very
good when made in advance,
even the day before.

1. Put the cabbage, apple,
celery, raisins and walnuts
into a bowl and mix well.
2. Mix together all the
dressing ingredients. Pour
into the bowl and mix
thoroughly.

Hot Potato Salad

SERVES 4

450 g (1 lb) waxy potatoes,
 peeled and diced
1 onion, peeled and chopped
1 tablespoon boiling water
1 tablespoon white wine
 vinegar
3 tablespoons mayonnaise
2 tablespoons single cream
salt
freshly ground black pepper
1 tablespoon chopped fresh
 parsley

PREPARATION TIME: *10 minutes*

COOKING TIME: *10-15 minutes*

1. Boil the potatoes in salted
water until just cooked.
2. Put the onion into a bowl,
add the boiling water and
vinegar.
3. Strain the potatoes, add to
the onion with the
mayonnaise, cream, salt and
pepper. Reheat gently if
necessary.
4. Serve sprinkled with
chopped parsley.

Chestnut Mousse

SERVES 4

2 eggs, separated
150 ml (¼ pint) milk
2 teaspoons powdered gelatine
2 tablespoons water
1 x 225 g (8 oz) can sweetened
 chestnut purée
150 ml (¼ pint) double cream
85 ml (3 fl oz) double cream,
 whipped, to decorate

PREPARATION TIME: *15 minutes,*
 plus setting

COOKING TIME: *10-15 minutes*

1. Put the egg yolks and milk
into a bowl over a pan of hot
water. Stir constantly until the
mixture thickens and coats
the back of a spoon. Do not
let the water boil.
2. Dissolve the gelatine in
the water over a gentle heat.
Beat into the purée together
with the custard. Cool
slightly, then add the cream.
3. Whisk the egg whites until
stiff, then lightly fold into the
chestnut mixture. Place in 4
small dishes. Chill until set.
4. Top with a teaspoonful of
cream.

Evening Meal
FEBRUARY

SMOKED MACKEREL HOT-POTS

TURKEY AND BROCCOLI LOAF
WITH MUSHROOM SAUCE

BAKED JACKET POTATOES

RHUBARB AND LEMON FLAN

Smoked Mackerel Hot-Pots

SERVES 4-6

15 g (½ oz) butter
2 sticks celery, chopped
1 small onion, peeled and
 chopped
225 g (8 oz) smoked mackerel
 fillets, skinned and flaked
2 tomatoes, skinned, seeded
 and chopped
juice of ½ lemon
2 tablespoons single cream
freshly ground black pepper
25 g (1 oz) brown breadcrumbs
25 g (1 oz) Cheddar cheese,
 finely grated
parsley sprigs, to garnish

PREPARATION TIME:	*15 minutes*
COOKING TIME:	*20-25 minutes*
OVEN:	*180°C, 350°F, Gas Mark 4*

1. Melt the butter in a small pan, fry the celery and onion until soft but not brown. Cool slightly.
2. Put the smoked mackerel in a bowl, add the tomatoes, lemon juice, cream, pepper, celery and onion.
3. Either divide the mixture between 4 ramekin dishes or place in 1 large ovenproof dish.
4. Mix together the breadcrumbs and cheese. Sprinkle the mixture evenly over each of the ramekin dishes or sprinkle evenly all over the large dish.
5. Place in a preheated oven for 20-25 minutes. Garnish with parsley sprigs.

Turkey and Broccoli Loaf

SERVES 4

50 g (2 oz) button mushrooms,
*   sliced*
15 g (½ oz) butter
225 g (8 oz) raw turkey breast,
*   minced*
225 g (8 oz) raw dark turkey
*   meat, minced*
1 onion, peeled and minced
50 g (2 oz) fresh white
*   breadcrumbs*
2 small eggs, beaten
2 tablespoons double cream
pinch of dried tarragon
salt
freshly ground black pepper
100 g (4 oz) broccoli spears,
*   lightly cooked*

SAUCE:

15 g (½ oz) butter
50 g (2 oz) mushrooms,
*   chopped*
15 g (½ oz) flour
150 ml (¼ pint) chicken stock
150 ml (¼ pint) milk
salt
freshly ground black pepper

PREPARATION TIME: *20 minutes*

COOKING TIME: *1½-1¾ hours*

OVEN: *180°C, 350°F, Gas Mark 4*

1. Lightly fry the mushrooms in the butter, then put them in an overlapping line down the centre of a well-greased 450 g (1 lb) loaf tin.
2. In a large bowl mix together the turkey, onion, breadcrumbs, eggs, cream, tarragon, salt and pepper.
3. Put half the mixture into the loaf tin. Put in the broccoli spears, then top with the remaining mixture. Cover with foil, then place in a roasting pan filled with boiling water. Place in a preheated oven for 1¼-1½ hours.
4. Meanwhile, make the sauce. Melt the butter in a pan, add the mushrooms and fry lightly. Stir in the flour and cook for 2-3 minutes.
5. Add the stock and milk gradually, then salt and pepper to taste. Bring to the boil and cook for 2-3 minutes.
6. When the loaf is cooked, turn it out of the tin and serve sliced with the mushroom sauce. Accompany with baked jacket potatoes.

Rhubarb and Lemon Flan

SERVES 4-6

175 g (6 oz) plain flour, sifted
75 g (3 oz) white cooking fat or
*   lard*
2-3 tablespoons water
450 g (1 lb) rhubarb, cut into
*   2.5 cm (1 inch) lengths*
1 egg
175 g (6 oz) caster sugar
25 g (1 oz) cornflour
25 g (1 oz) butter
grated rind of 1 lemon
juice of 1 lemon made up to
*   150 ml (¼ pint) with water*

PREPARATION TIME: *20 minutes,*
*   plus chilling*

COOKING TIME: *40 minutes*

OVEN: *180°C, 350°F, Gas Mark 4;*
*   200°C, 400°F, Gas Mark 5*

The forced rhubarb that is in the shops around February is quite tender, however later in the season the main crop tends to be a bit tougher and therefore will need peeling before use. The flan can go in the oven with the loaf, while cooking at the lower temperature.

1. Put the flour into a bowl and rub in the fat until the mixture resembles breadcrumbs. Add the water and mix to a soft dough. Chill for 30 minutes.
2. Roll out the pastry and line a 25 cm (10 inch) flan tin.
3. Arrange the rhubarb in circles in the flan tin.
4. Put the egg, sugar, cornflour, butter, lemon rind, lemon juice and water in a pan. Bring to the boil slowly, stirring all the time.
5. Spread the lemon mixture over the rhubarb. Place in a preheated oven for 30 minutes, then increase the heat for a further 15 minutes. Serve warm.

VARIATION:

This flan can be made with orange instead of lemon. Follow the recipe but reduce the amount of sugar to 100 g (4 oz) and add ½ teaspoon ground ginger, if liked.

Prue Leith's Dinner Party

FEBRUARY

LEEK TERRINE WITH WALNUTS AND FETA

PLAITED TURBOT AND TROUT WITH
TARRAGON BUTTER SAUCE

FRENCH BAKED PEAS

CHAMPAGNE WATER-ICE

This menu is pretty to look at, and light and untaxing to eat. However, it requires careful cooking and the beurre montée sauce and poached fish need some last-minute effort from the cook. The first and last courses can be made in advance. Even week-old flat champagne makes astonishingly good sorbet, but any white wine, still or sparkling, will do.

Leek Terrine with walnuts and feta
(recipe page 140)

Leek Terrine with Walnuts and Feta

SERVES 6

20 small young leeks
radiccio or other chicory leaves
75 g (3 oz) feta, crumbled
50 g (2 oz) walnuts, chopped
sea salt
freshly ground black pepper

DRESSING:

4 tablespoons olive oil
2 tablespoons walnut oil
2 tablespoons wine vinegar
2 tablespoons English mustard
salt
freshly ground black pepper

PREPARATION TIME: *25 minutes, plus chilling*

COOKING TIME: *10 minutes*

It is important to use tender young leeks and the radiccio leaves provide a good colour.

1. Cut off the roots and most of the green part of the leeks. Split the leeks horizontally to within 5 cm (2 inches) of the root end. Riffle the leaves under a running cold tap to wash out any grit or mud.
2. Boil the leeks in salted water for 10 minutes or until tender.
3. Fill a 450 g (1 lb) loaf tin with the leeks laid head to tail alternately, sprinkling each layer with salt and pepper. Put another tin inside the first, pressing down the leeks. Invert both tins so that the water can drain out. Chill for at least 4 hours with a 1 kg (2 lb) weight on top.
4. Carefully turn out the leek terrine. Using a very sharp knife, slice into 6 thick slices. Lay each slice on a plate and surround with the salad leaves. Scatter the walnuts and crushed feta cheese on top of the salad.
5. Combine the dressing ingredients, add salt and pepper and spoon over the terrine.
(Pictured on page 139.)

Plaited turbot and trout with tarragon butter sauce; French baked peas

Plaited Turbot and Trout with Tarragon Butter Sauce

SERVES 6

1.4 kg (3 lb) pink trout or
  salmon fillet, skinned
750 g (1½ lb) turbot or any
  firm white fish fillet, skinned

STOCK:

85 ml (3 fl oz) white wine
1 carrot, peeled and shredded
1 leek, peeled and shredded
1 onion, peeled and sliced
1 bay leaf
good bunch of parsley
fish heads, bones and skins
1.2 litres (2 pints) water
12 peppercorns
pinch of salt

SAUCE:

300 ml (½ pint) reduced fish
  stock
150 g (5 oz) butter, chilled
1 teaspoon flour
2 tablespoons double cream
1 tablespoon chopped tarragon
salt
freshly ground black pepper

PREPARATION TIME: *40 minutes*

COOKING TIME: *about 1 hour*

OVEN: *180°C, 350°F, Gas Mark 4*

1. As you are going to plait the fish into elegant bi-coloured ropes you need neat strips of flesh. There may be some waste, but odd pieces can be cooked with the plaits and used up later.
2. Cut the pink fish (salmon or trout) into 12 strips 18 cm (7 inches) long, 1 cm (½ inch) thick, and 1 cm (½ inch) wide. Cut the white fish into 6 similar pieces.
3. Make 6 neat plaits, using 2 pink and 1 white fish strip for each one, and lay neatly in a roasting tin.
4. Boil the stock ingredients together for 30 minutes. Strain.
5. Pour the stock over the fish and poach very gently in a preheated oven until just firm. Lift out carefully and dish up on a serving platter. Keep covered.
6. Reduce the stock by boiling down to 300 ml (½ pint).
7. Melt 25 g (1 oz) of the butter in a sloping-sided, small, heavy saucepan and stir in the flour. Add the reduced stock and stir until boiling. You should have a barely thickened sauce.
8. Cut the remaining butter into small dice and whisk it, one piece at a time into the boiling sauce; it will form an emulsion. Keep whisking and adding butter until it is all incorporated.
9. Add the cream and tarragon. Taste, season and pour round the fish.
10. Serve with French baked peas (see next page).

NOTE:

For this elegant dish you need pieces of fish which are at least 18 cm (7 inches) long, so bear this in mind when choosing. Once the plaits are cooked, they are very delicate, so handle them with care.

Champagne Water-Ice

SERVES 6

225 g (8 oz) sugar
300 ml (½ pint) water
300 ml (½ pint) champagne
juice of 1 lemon and 1 orange

PREPARATION TIME: *15 minutes,*
plus freezing

A water-ice is quick and simple to make, being basically a sugar syrup flavoured with fruit juice and then frozen. The addition of alcohol means that the ice will melt very quickly at room temperature, so leave it in the freezer until just before serving.

1. Set the freezer to coldest. If making the water-ice without a processor or sorbetière, put a bowl and whisk into the freezer to chill. If using a processor for the whisking, freeze the mixture in ice-cube trays and, when rock-solid, process the cubes to smoothness.
2. Dissolve the sugar in the water. Add the champagne and fruit juices. Pour into shallow trays and freeze. When frozen round the edges but still soft in the centre, tip into the chilled bowl and whisk until smooth. Refreeze.
3. Repeat the whisking at intervals until creamy, smooth and white.
4. Chill serving glasses or bowls before dinner.

French Baked Peas

SERVES 6

½ large mild Spanish onion,
peeled and thinly sliced
1 garlic clove, peeled and
crushed
2 sprigs of mint
50 g (2 oz) butter
1 teaspoon sugar
6 large outside leaves of lettuce
or 1 small lettuce, shredded
750 g (1½ lb) small frozen or
fresh peas

PREPARATION TIME: *15 minutes*

COOKING TIME: *1½-2 hours*

OVEN: *160°C, 325°F, Gas Mark 3*

1. Put the sliced onion, garlic, mint, butter, sugar and shredded lettuce in an oven-to-table casserole. Add the peas. (If using fresh peas add ½ cup water to the casserole.)
2. Cover the casserole with foil and bake in a preheated oven for 1½-2 hours until the onions are tender. Stir once during cooking to mix the flavours.

Champagne water ice

FOOD PREPARED FOR PHOTOGRAPHY BY:
Jacki Baxter
Jackie Burrow
Lisa Collard
Clare Gordon-Smith
Hilary Foster
Heather Lambert
Michelle Thomson
DESIGN:
Millions Design

ACKNOWLEDGEMENTS

PHOTOGRAPHY:
Laurie Evans
Christine Hanscomb
PHOTOGRAPHIC STYLING:
Antonia Gaunt
Lesley Richardson